New Essays in

Philosophy of Mind

Series II

Edited by
David Copp and J.J. MacIntosh

Guelph, Ontario
1985

Produced for the C.A.P.P. by The University of Calgary Press

ISSN 0045-5091 ISBN 0-919491-11-1

Table of Contents

CANADIAN JOURNAL OF PHILOSOPHY
Supplementary Volume 11

Introduction

J.J. MacINTOSH
University of Calgary

This year's *C.J.P.* supplementary volume consists of ten papers in the philosophy of mind, an area that is as difficult to delineate as any other philosophical area.

G.E. Moore used to answer the question, 'What is philosophy?', by pointing to the books on his shelves and saying, 'Philosophy is what these books are about.' Philosophy of mind is what *some* of those books are about, and its enquiries frequently move into neighbouring areas, with logic, semantics, neurophysiology, literature, epistemology and metaphysics providing some obvious examples, as the papers in this collection reveal.

Though it is hard to say *exactly* what 'philosophy of mind' encompasses there are some issues which are clearly central. Here are three questions concerning 'minds' – 'souls, actually,' one of our contributors (Sharvy) suggests, nicely achieving today's shock value with yesterday's truism – which have loomed large in our questionings about ourselves.

(1) What is the relation between the world we perceive and our perceptions of it?

(2) What is the relation between mental events/processes/states and events/processes/states in the brain?

(3) What is the connection between mental faculties (especially memory) and personal identity?

In the area between philosophy of mind and ethics comes the further question, too seldom asked.

(4) What are the moral restrictions on our inner lives: are there things we ought not to do, even in thought?

The language in which these questions are couched is question-begging and could easily be made more so without moving away from what are still standard idioms within the field. Descartes must bear some of the blame for this, since many of the misleading assumptions embedded in our vocabulary are indeed his, even if not his alone, and have been entrenched there because of his deserved popularity and influence.

Therefore, and without wishing to play down the degree of continuity between Descartes and his mediaeval and renaissance predecessors, I offer the following three debilitating doctrines as *Descartes' legacy*:

(1) That *idea* – a term labelling distinct, individuable entities – should be one of the primitive terms in philosophy of mind and epistemology. By extension, that we can make sense of hoping, choosing, fearing, intending, etc., in a vocabulary rich in count nouns. Further, remembering the sentential function of 'idea' in Descartes and Spinoza, it is easy to see that this doctrine must bear at least part of the responsibility for the development of the sorts of sentential epistemology which we shall find Churchland deprecating.

(2) That at least some of these *ideas* are non-physical, and not located in the brain. By extension, that we need an account of the relation between our 'ideas' and the workings of our brains.

(3) That the explanation of our abilities to indulge in certain sorts of ratiocination, as well as our ability to behave in a non-stereotyped way (particularly when the behaviour in question is linguistic) is not to be sought in terms of brain-centred explanations. By extension, that with respect to humans ('free' 'rational' 'agents'), 'animal' is a phase sortal and 'person' is the substance sortal rather than the other way around, and that, in consequence, *personal* identity poses a different problem from (say) oyster identity, or from that of the identity of human animals, viewed as members of a particular biological species.

For some of us, all three of these suggestions are totally implausible, but a glance at the literature shows their ubiquity and, like prejudices acquired unwittingly in childhood, they are likely to colour our views without our noticing their influence.

Since I blame them, in part at least, on Descartes, it is worth reminding ourselves that, for Descartes, a large part of what *we* label the mental was unproblematically physical. In particular, staying well within the tradition of such writers as Roger Bacon, da Vinci, and Kepler, Descartes held that *images* (which he sometimes calls *ideas*) were spatio-temporal items located in the brain, and that, in consequence, non-corporeal entities such as the angels would not have an imaginative faculty. There is also, clearly, a problem for *us* in the putative after-life, given that Descartes thinks that memory of particular events is also corporeal. Descartes recognizes this problem but conspicuously fails to solve it.

Memory becomes a more acute problem when, with Locke – though not with his more scientifically minded contemporaries, Boyle and Hooke – Descartes' partial physicalism begins to be dropped, and the problems that we try to solve in terms of functionalism, e.g., begin to arise.

For people within the pre-Lockean tradition memory need not pose a particular problem, for the memory images are simply stored in the brain (Hooke even offers us a calculation to show that there is plenty of space available). There is, of course, *our* problem of connecting the top-down and the bottom-up stories. However, for philosophers such as Locke, Berkeley and Hume there is an *extra* problem or set of problems.

The problem arises when we try, with Locke, to combine the things we want and need to say about remembering, particularly if we try to couch our remarks in the *ideas* terminology, with a thorough going (non-Cartesian) dualism in which we regard *all* ideas/images as purely mental entities. This, as McIntyre points out in 'The Connection Between Impressions and Ideas' was the bind Locke landed himself in, for on the one hand he uses the language of common sense (ideas are *re*called) and of the earlier scientific tradition (so that images come into the mind from outside), while on the other (partly, McIntyre suggests, in order to accommodate his doctrine of personal identity) he makes ideas totally mind-based (so that they are evanescent and can only be 'as it were' recalled).

Realizing that there was a problem with the 'idea' terminology, but being unwilling or unable to scrap it completely, Hume attempted to sort things out by adding a distinction between ideas and impressions but this, McIntyre argues, proved insufficient to deal with all of Hume's problems, some of which were inherent in bits of doctrine he took over, but some of which were self-inflicted.

For example, in a manner reminiscent of Spinoza before him, Hume wanted an *intrinsic* difference between memory and non-memory images. Moreover, given the fact that Hume's theory of personal identity is such a heavy drawer on the memory bank, and given Hume's views about causality, it is implausible to argue, McIntyre suggests, that any causal theory of memory can be constructed to save the (or a) Humean position, particularly since Hume explicitly disavows the possibility of continuing inherence of the memory images in 'something simple and individual.'

One of the problems with the Humean position lies in Hume's acceptance of the *idea* terminology, and in 'Reid on Testimony and Perception' Lehrer and Smith offer us an interesting and sympathetic account of Reid's rejection of such an account, and his attempt to redo the analysis within a semantic framework, offering Reid to us, plausibly enough, as a sort of materialistic Berkeley, someone who keeps both the linguistic elements of Berkeley's philosophy of nature, and his decisive rejection of Locke's resemblance account of primary qualities.

The doctrine on which Reid relies heavily, that like effects are produced by like causes, has considerably less plausibility than its converse, even within the limited sphere in which he employs it, but Lehrer and Smith are surely right in suggesting that the results he gets by adding this doctrine to his general account of first principles and of natural signs deserve more respect and attention than they generally receive.

Contemporary answers to the questions posed earlier continue to be haunted by the ghosts of ideas but are, in the main, squarely in the camp of what earlier thinkers would have regarded as materialism. Since Ryle, of course, we have less interest in such 'ism'ing, and indeed the issues are more subtle than such labels allow.

In 'Searle on Programs and Intentionality' Sharvy, distinguishing between the strong and the weak sense of 'instantiating' ('following,' 'obeying') takes Searle's Chinese room puzzle and offers us a more cautious but also, as he believes, a more correct account of the relation between computing and intentionality. His startling claim in note 4 will, I trust, lead many readers to his *Teaching Philosophy* article.

Worries about intentionality also provide the starting point for Lyons's 'Dennett, Functionalism, and Introspection,' but though he touches on the Searle problem, he is primarily interested in the version(s) of functionalism that Dennett has offered. Dennett's writings on this topic represent one of the strongest cases for functionalism, and Lyons's balanced and careful unveiling of the difficulties Dennett's views face, particularly with respect to the question of introspection, show how difficult the matter is for anyone who wants to take a Dennett-like line.

Levin looks at another attack on functionalism, one which results from adapting Kripke's 'conceivability' attack on the identity thesis to the case of functionalism. In a way that is not open to the identity theorist, she argues, the functionalist can plausibly deny that there are any 'conceivability' counter-examples to functionalism as properly understood.

It is not the case, she claims, 'that, for any functional description [of one of our states], we can imagine or conceive of a being that satisfies it, yet is unable to feel what we feel [when in the state in question.]'

This strong claim leads her into very interesting, if murky, Leibnizian waters, particularly since she is clear that (a) we do not currently have correct functional descriptions of our states, and (b) such descriptions must eventually come from the empirical sciences. Her paper and Churchland's make an interesting pair.

The next three papers consist of attacks on a pair of theses which Paul Churchland has espoused, plus his reply to them. The first thesis is that of eliminative materialism, the second concerns the semantics of sensation terms.

In 'A Materialist's Misgivings About Eliminative Materialism' Foss offers himself, by implicature at least, as an embarrassed materialist (surely one of this volume's least plausible claims; Fossian embarrassment is to real embarrassment, I suspect, much as Cartesian doubt is to real doubt), and offers us reasons why such embarrassment is appropriate, at least for an *eliminative* materialist.

Thurston and Coval, in their subtle and closely argued 'Sensation, Theory and Meaning' look at the difficulties which arise for someone like Churchland (or earlier, for someone like J.J.C. Smart, say, who reaches the same conclusion by a different route) who wants to suggest that the phenomenological aspect of sensation terms may be, as far as meaning goes, totally ignored.

In his reply Churchland suggests, *contra* Foss, that it is only a considerably more extreme kind of eliminative materialism than he either needs or wishes to avow that should cause Fossian embarassment. With respect to Thurston and Coval, too, he argues that the differences may, by and large, be more apparent than real, with the final difference being merely 'residual.'

He remains firmly committed, however, to the view that for us as 'epistemic engines,' sensations are not essential either 'semantically or epistemologically.' It does seem that such epistemic engines are conceivable (though Levin might disagree) and as Churchland points out, the phenomenon of blind-sight provides us with a partial case. This remains true, incidentally, even if recent attempts to explain blind-sight in terms of light scattering, threshold effects, and remaining striate cortex win out over the earlier 'mid brain' explanatory story.

There is, as both parties to the dispute would undoubtedly agree, more — much more — to be said on both sides of this discussion, and it is to be hoped that the debate will continue.

With Cherry's 'The Inward and the Outward: Fantasy, Reality and

Satisfaction' we return to the topic of imagination, but to a function of imagination that seems not to have attracted a great deal of philosophical attention in the past. This is the question of the use of imagination in achieving real or surrogate ends through day-dreaming or fantasizing, and the further, associated questions which arise concerning the moral evaluation of such fantasizing.

At the far end of one evaluation spectrum we have the clearly immoral (though why, *exactly*?) drug induced fantasies of *Brave New World*; at the near end of one advice spectrum we have Rousseau endorsing the stoical views that we should starve the imagination in order to reduce the frustration resulting from the reality/fantasy gap.

Cherry concentrates on a more difficult, intermediate area: can I demean or harm myself by my fantasizing and, more difficult still, can I demean or harm *you*, through having you as a figure playing a particular role in my fantasies? We know that many 'demeaning' fantasies can have desirable or desired *immediate* effects (their role for many people in reaching orgasm provides an obvious case) but are the long term effects equally acceptable? – and what about their *intrinsic* desirability? Again, this is a fruitful area that deserves more attention than it gets.

With 'Amnesia and Psychological Continuity' Brennan brings us back to the role of memory in personal identity, but with a look at forgetting as well as at remembering. By concentrating on real cases of amnesia he performs at least two services for us. He reminds us, salutorily, of how various the human animal is, and how unwise it is to tie personhood, a priori, to the possession of a long term memory. Further, looking at such cases reveals an ambiguity in the accepted account of 'continuity' which has vitiated some recent discussions of personal identity.

CANADIAN JOURNAL OF PHILOSOPHY
Supplementary Volume 11

*The Connection Between Impressions and Ideas**

JANE L. McINTYRE
Cleveland State University
Cleveland, OH 44115
U.S.A.

I. Introduction

Hume contributed to the theory of ideas by distinguishing impressions from ideas. This refinement of Locke's theory is usually held to be a clarification of Locke's broad use of the term 'idea,' and yet the distinction has remained problematic. The bifurcation of the Lockean realm of ideas necessitated an explanation of the relations between the newly named entities. The most basic aspects of this relationship, as

---

* A version of this paper was read at the Eleventh Hume Congress, Toronto, Canada, August 1982.

presented in the *Treatise*,[1] are that impressions cause ideas and that ideas represent impressions. In this paper I will argue that Hume's theory cannot accommodate the claim that impressions cause ideas, and that this fundamental inability to trace the causal history of an idea is the source of several other problems in Hume's philosophy of mind. I will begin by outlining two such problems that Hume's theory faces. I will then argue that in each case the fundamental difficulty concerns the causal connection between impressions and ideas. In conclusion, I will briefly argue that this same problem is implicit Locke, and therefore represents a basic weakness in the general framework of the theory of ideas itself.

II. A Problem About Memory

For Hume, memories fall into a category somewhat between impressions and ideas. All simple ideas are caused by impressions, and resemble them (*T* 4f.). The complex ideas of memory are distinguished from other ideas by their force and vivacity (*T* 85). This is the same characteristic that separates impressions from ideas generally. In fact, at times Hume seems to be indifferent to the question of whether memories count as ideas or impressions. Book I, Part III, Section 5 of the *Treatise* uses both terms. Both this section and Book I, Part I, Section 3 suggest that impressions gradually fade and decay, remaining memories so long as they retain sufficient vivacity to cause belief. However, this process can be reversed, with ideas regaining vivacity. In the Appendix Hume describes the case of a man whose memory is revived by hearing a friend tell of a past event:

> Here the person that forgets receives at first all the ideas from the discourse of the other, with the same circumstances of time and place; tho' he considers them as mere fictions of the imagination. But as soon as the cir-

---

1 David Hume, *A Treatise of Human Nature*, edited by Selby-Bigge; second edition edited by P.H. Nidditch (Oxford: Oxford University Press 1978). All references to the *Treatise* are to this edition, and will be given in the body of the paper.

> cumstance is mention'd, that touches the memory, the very same ideas now appear in a new light, and have, in a manner, a different feeling from what they had before. Without any other alteration, beside that of the feeling, they become immediately ideas of the memory, and are assented to. (*T* 628)

It also appears that *any* idea can take on the feeling characteristic of memory. Hume says,

> ... an idea of the imagination may acquire such a force and vivacity, as to pass for an idea of the memory, and counterfeit its effects on the belief and judgment. This is noted in the case of liars; who by the frequent repetition of their lies, come at last to believe and remember them, as realities. (*T* 86)

The very characteristic that Hume appeals to in order to explain the difference between ideas of memory and those of imagination can become attached to ideas that are not of realities. What, if anything, will distinguish the veridical memory experiences from those of the liar with the vivid imagination?

One obstacle to providing an adequate answer to this question is that Hume *rejects* an appeal to the relationship between an idea and its antecedent impression to explain how we distinguish, generally, between memory and imagination. Such a distinction, he feels, must be based on intrinsic characteristics of the perceptions themselves (*T* 85). But although from an internal perspective we cannot separate memory from mere idea except by their degrees of force, Hume *did* hold that memories could be counterfeited. Therefore, there must be more to Hume's concept of memory than that of a forceful idea, even if relative vivacity is our only guide to the difference between memories and other ideas.[2] Given Hume's acceptance of the possibility of counterfeit memories, forcefulness is a necessary but not a sufficient condition for an idea being a true memory. However, problems arise as soon as we attempt to spell out the conditions that would be sufficient.

It might be thought that veridical memory could be adequately

2 Noxon argues that Hume has a double standard for distinguishing the ideas of memory from those of the imagination. See James Noxon, 'Remembering and Imagining the Past,' in D.W. Livingston and J.T. King (eds.), *Hume: A Re-evaluation* (New York: Fordham University Press 1976), 270-95.

characterized in the following way: true memories are those apparent memories which have been preceded by impressions similar in the content and order of events. Such precedence alone, however, is not enough. The liar with the lively imagination may have, in a sense, appropriated the actions of another. The events he believes himself to have done may have been done – but by someone else. Nor can we say that the preceding similar impressions must have occured in the same bundle of perceptions, for bundles of perceptions are individuated, in part, on the basis of the existence of memory relations between ideas and impressions.

We can attempt to strengthen the precedence-condition by stipulating that the apparent memory must be *caused* by a similar impression. Can Hume's theory of ideas incorporate this very intuitive suggestion? I think not. First, the memory and the original impression are not contiguous. In such cases a causal connection can only exist if a chain of causes and effects connects the non-contiguous events (*T* 75). Remembering, however, does not seem to have this character. The scent of orange blossoms prompts memories (in me) of a place in California where I was several years ago. The scent and the place are associated, and so the impression of one prompts the image of the other. But the cause of the memory-image is the present scent of flowers. That scent arises from causes external to me, and not from whatever perceptions preceded it. There is no chain of causes back to the original impression.

There are several ways of trying to remedy this situation in the context of a Humean theory. It might be arguèd that the propensity to associate that scent and that image provides the required continous link between the original impression and the later memory of it. Dispositions, customs and propensities do, of course, play an important role in Hume's account of human nature. But on Hume's theory of mind they cannot have an existence over and above that of perceptions. On a Humean account of propensities, such as that suggested by Stroud, a propensity exists in a mind if certain conditional statements hold true with respect to the bundle of perceptions that constitutes it.[3] On such an account the propensity to associate a scent and an image is

3 Barry Stroud, *Hume* (London: Routledge and Kegan Paul 1977), 131

merely the conditional fact that if the scent occurs, the image occurs. Unless particular propensities are reified, as I do not think Hume would do, they cannot fill in the gap beteen the past impression and the present memory. Propensities, on this view are really more descriptive than explanatory.

Another approach to this problem, one which I think would be favored by Bricke, would be to have states of the body fill in the causal gaps between perceptions.[4] However, this suggestion too appears unsatisfactory. Although much in Hume's discussion of personal identity is unclear and subject to dispute, he is clearest in his rejection of the view that the perceptions which constitute a self are related by inhering in a substance. In Book I, Part IV, Section 6, he says:

> The mind is a kind of theatre, where several perceptions successively make their appearance ... The comparison of the theatre must not mislead us. They are the successive perceptions only, that constitute the mind; nor have we the most distant notion of the place, where these scenes are represented, or of the materials, of which it is compos'd. (*T* 253)

And in the Appendix,

> Did our perceptions ... inhere in something simple and individual ... there would be no difficulty in the case. (*T* 636)

If bodily states are required to connect memories and the impressions they are derived from, then the perceptions of the mind, taken alone, are *not* connected to each other, and it is not the perceptions only which would constitute the mind. Rather, as in the interpretation of the theater example which Hume rejects, it would be the association of perceptions with something else (the body) which would explain their connection.

Hume's various discussions of memory bring out an equivocal aspect of his treatment of the nature of impressions and ideas. As noted earlier, he speaks of impressions as decaying (*T* 85), wearing out

---

4 John Bricke, 'Hume on Self Identity, Memory and Causality,' in G.P. Morice (ed.), *David Hume: Bicentenary Papers* (Austin: University of Texas Press 1977), 172

(*T* 86), of impressions degenerating into ideas (*T* 86), and of ideas gaining and losing vivacity (*T* 85, 86, 628). Similarly, in his discussion of personal identity, when speaking (admittedly strangely) of seeing 'clearly into the breast of another' he says ... 'and suppose that he always preserves the memory of a considerable part of his past perceptions' (*T* 260). These references clearly suggest that persistence of perceptions when not perceived. The persistence of perceptions would allow for the existence of causal connections between the ideas of memory and earlier impressions. This would enable Hume's theory to maintain a distinction between veridical and counterfeit memories, as he wishes to do. However, Hume held that impressions are 'internal and perishing existences' (*T* 194). Perceptions are 'removed by sleep' and the self does not exist at that time (*T* 252). In fact, continued existence is taken as one of the characteristics definitive of independence from perception (*T* 188). The persistence of perceptions required by an account of veridical memory, and suggested by the language Hume uses in his discussion of memory, is not compatible with his more explicit statements about the nature of impressions and ideas.

III. A Problem About Personal Identity

In a recent analysis of Hume's doubts about his account of personal identity, Garrett presents the following argument.[5] Qualitatively identical perceptions could differ in their causal relationships only by differing in spatial and/or temporal location. According to Hume, some perceptions have no spatial location – they can exist 'and yet be no where' (*T* 235f.). Suppose two bundles of perceptions (two minds) contained qualitatively identical impressions of this non-spatial sort at one time. (Not all the component perceptions would have to be identical for this to be true.) The the causal relationships of those qualitatively identical perceptions would also have to be identical – they would differ in no causally relevant respect. Therefore, there

5 Don Garrett, 'Hume's Self-Doubts About Personal Identity,' *The Philosophical Review*, XC, No. 3 (1981), 337-58

would be no way, on Hume's theory, to explain why some subsequent idea of such an impression was connected to one bundle rather than the other. According to Hume, causation and resemblance are the principles that are supposed to unite perceptions into bundles through time. Here, however, we have a clear case where those principles would fail.

An example can illustrate this point. Reversing the case of memory described earlier, suppose that a picture of a place in California evokes (in me) an idea of the scent of orange blossoms. At the time I experienced that scent others did too – and so at that time more than one bundle of perceptions contained an impression of the scent of orange blossoms. The idea I have now is a distinct existent, with no real (or necessary) connection to any other idea (*T* 636). We can see that resemblance alone cannot account for the connection between my idea and just *one* impression in the past, for my idea resembles all those earlier impressions. However, the connection will also fail to be explained by an appeal to causation. For, given their qualitative identity, the fact that they exist at the same time, and the fact that they have no spatial co-ordinates, no *one* impression would have any feature not also shared by the others. Therefore, no one impression of the scent of orange blossoms could be singled out as the cause of my idea. This entails that no link exists between this present bundle of perceptions and a unique bundle at that past time.

It might be thought, at first, that the consequences of Garrett's argument could be avoided in the following way. *My* impression of the scent of orange blossoms was preceded by a particular set of perceptions. These relationships to other perceptions will distinguish between my impressions and the others, providing a unique feature by which to single out the cause of my idea. But this argument would beg the question. The ideas preceding my impression have no necessary connection to it. They stand in the same relation of precedence to *all* the other impressions occurring at that time, and therefore they provide no unique characterization of *my* impression. Needless to say, the same argument would apply against any attempt to appeal to my other perceptions occurring at the same time as the scent of orange blossoms.

A consideration of Garrett's argument also provides a further reason why the previously mentioned reconstruction of Hume's theory of mind suggested by Bricke would not solve this fundamental problem about causality. On Bricke's view, bodily states can fill the gaps between perceptions. However, if qualitatively identical, non-spatial perceptions occurred at the same time, Garrett's argument shows that there would be no reason for the perceptions to be associated with the states of one body rather than another. There is no way such perceptions could differ in any of their causal relationships, whether with respect to bodily states or to other perceptions.

IV. Conclusion

The problems discussed in Parts II and III of this paper reveal a serious flaw in Hume's account of the connections between impressions and ideas. In the *Treatise* ideas are intended to stand in *both* representative and causal relations to impressions. In the case of memory and in the case of personal identity we have seen that resemblance (a relationship of representation) alone is too weak to explain how a particular idea is related to a particular earlier impression: ideas resemble many impressions from which we would not say they are derived. But Hume's account of causation is not adequate to the task of tightening the bond between impressions and ideas. The discussion of memory has shown that so long as contiguity (whether direct or mediated) is required for causal connections, Hume's view that perceptions do not persist unperceived undermines the basic claim that impressions are the cause of ideas. And the discussion of personal identity has shown that Hume's account of causality does not permit causally distinct roles for simultaneous qualitatively identical impressions. Yet without this, no sense can be made of past impressions belonging to a present bundle of perceptions.

I have argued that one of Hume's most fundamental tenets about the relationship between impressions and ideas cannot be supported in the context of the arguments presented in the *Treatise*. I will now briefly indicate the way in which this problem appears to me to be prefigured in Locke's *Essay Concerning Human Understanding.*[6] Locke's

---

6 John Locke, *An Essay Concerning Human Understanding*, ed. P.H. Nidditch

main discussion of memory occurs in Book II, Chapter X, of the *Essay*. Locke speaks of ideas as being 'out of sight' (*Essay* 149) or 'dormant' (*Essay* 153), of memory being a 'Store-house' or 'Repository' (*Essay* 150). He also speaks, as Hume later did, of ideas decaying (*Essay* 151) and fading (*Essay* 152). In contrast to the *Treatise*, the dominant view of memory in the *Essay* is that of a place where ideas may exist without being contemplated, a place in which they may change and deteriorate, and from which ideas may even entirely disappear (*Essay* 153). Locke attributes some defects of memory to defects of the body (*Essay* 153) and although in Chapter I of Book II he rejects the view that there is a necessary connection between memory and the body, he does seem to argue that the soul does not, as a matter of fact, have a memory apart from its body (*Essay* 112-13).

In the second edition of the *Essay*, at the same time that he added the chapter discussing personal identity, Locke added several lengthy comments to the chapter on memory. As is well known, Locke traced personal identity via 'continuity of consciousness,' with memory providing the essential links. Locke's account of personal identity rejects the view that the identity of a person depends upon the identity of an underlying substance. In this context, it is interesting to note that Locke inserted the following comment into his discussion of memory. After a sentence calling the memory a repository of ideas, Locke added in the second edition:

> But our *Ideas* being nothing, but actual Perceptions in the Mind, which cease to be any thing, when there is no perception of them, this *laying up* of our *Ideas* in the Repository of the Memory, signifies no more but this, that the Mind has a Power, in many cases, to revive Perceptions, which it once had, with this additional Perception annexed to them, that it has had them before. And in this Sense it is, that our *Ideas* are said to be in our Memories, when indeed, they are actually no where, but only there is an ability in the Mind, when it will, to revive them again; and as it were to paint them anew on it self, though some with more, some with less difficulty; some more lively, and others more obscurely. (*Essay* 150. Italics in original.)

(Oxford: Oxford University Press 1975). All references to Locke are to this edition, and will be given in the body of the paper.

This new comment is a deviation from the original 'store-house' view of memory, as it explicitly states that ideas 'cease to be any thing, when there is no perception of them.' For Locke, all that marks these perceptions as memories is the feeling that they have been experienced before. And although this is, I think a real break with his earlier account of memory, it is more consistent with his new account of personal identity than the storehouse view; the latter carries the connotation that self *is* the storehouse, whether the items in it are accessible to consciousness or not.

Here we can see that the stage is set for the problem encountered in Hume. Ideas in memory are severed from continuity with the original experiences that gave rise to them. Memory therefore becomes exclusively a representational, and not a causal, relationship. In Locke, this problem has its origins in his rejection of the Cartesian view that the soul is a substance that always thinks (and hence which must think at times when we are not conscious). The move towards an empirical account of the self, defined by that with which we are acquainted in experience rather than inherence in an underlying substance, forced a parallel move away from the storehouse model of memory. Both these trends are an integral part of Hume's philosophy of mind – but they entail a problem about tracing the causal history of an idea. If ideas cease to exist when not in consciousness, the connections between ideas existing at different times can at best be that of resemblance. However, this is insufficient to account for veridical memory, as Locke himself implicitly acknowledged when he relied on the goodness of God to insure that consciousness of actions would never be transferred to individuals who had not performed those actions (*Essay* 337-8). That Locke was having difficulty with this aspect of his account of memory is also evidenced by his statement, once again added in the second edition:

> This farther is to be observed, concerning *Ideas* lodg'd in the Memory, and upon occasion revived by the Mind, that they are not only (as the Word *revive* imports) none of them new ones; but also that the Mind takes notice of them, as of a former Impression, and renews its acquaintance with them, as *Ideas* it had known before. So that though *Ideas* formerly imprinted are not all constantly in view, yet in remembrance they are constantly known to be such, as have been formerly imprinted, *i.e.* in view, and taken notice of before by the Understanding. (*Essay* 153. Italics in original.)

The word 'revive' does connote, as Locke said, something that is not new. However, this manner of speech is appropriate only if the memory is *literally* a repository of ideas. Locke's broad use of the term 'idea' may be helping him to avoid a problem here by enabling him to refer to the idea originally imprinted and the idea in memory as one continous thing, even though he was coming to regard them as separate. Hume's new terminology of 'impressions' and 'ideas'[7] clarified the theory of ideas, but also crystallized Locke's problem. If memory does not literally store ideas, if the idea is not a faded remnant of the impression that occurred earlier, but rather a new entity, then the connection between the original experience and the later idea remains to be explained. Hume maintained that impressions *cause* ideas. His own account of causality, however, makes this view untenable.

Received November, 1983

7 The quotation from page 153 shows that Locke also sometimes used the term 'impression' in a sense superficially like that of Hume. There are references throughout Book II, Chapter I of the *Essay* to ideas being imprinted, and to 'Impressions.' But in Locke, the term 'impression' usually signifies the way in which an idea is received, and not merely a forceful perception. See especially *Essay* 117.

CANADIAN JOURNAL OF PHILOSOPHY
Supplementary Volume 11

Reid on Testimony and Perception

KEITH LEHRER and JOHN-CHRISTIAN SMITH
The University of Arizona
Tucson, AZ 85721
U.S.A.

Reid defended common sense against scepticism by appeal to the claim that our faculties should be considered trustworthy until some argument proves them to be untrustworthy. He believed, of course, that no such argument would be forthcoming. In this paper, we shall investigate Reid's defense of the faculty of perception and the evidence of the senses by analogy with the faculty of language and the evidence of testimony. Reid argued that the evidence of testimony should be trusted unless there is reason to think it untrustworthy and by analogy, that the evidence of the senses should be trusted unless there is reason to think it untrustworthy. He admitted the fallibility of such evidence but contended that such fallibility is characteristic of all our faculties. Moreover, and perhaps most important, Reid developed a psychological theory of the faculties of perception and language that showed the analogy between these two faculties to be very exact indeed. We shall exhibit this analogy in order to elucidate Reid's psychology and epistemology. Our conclusions will thereby show that Reid's psychology is a very modern theory of cognitive information processing and that his epistemology based on this theory combines elements of reliability, first principles, and coherence as the ingredients of human knowledge.

Reply to the Ideal Theory

Reid's attack on scepticism is not directed against the total sceptic who accepts nothing but rather, against a tradition with ancient roots that has found a modern articulation in the tradition beginning with Descartes, developing through Locke and Berkeley, and culminating with Hume. The basic tenet of the *ideal theory* is that what is before the mind is always some idea or, as Hume says, impression. It is this doctrine that leads to scepticism, Reid claims, and he undertakes the refutation of this theory. In his defense of beliefs in the existence of the external world, Reid notes,

> ... that all mankind have a fixed belief of an external material world ... is likewise a fact, for which we have all the evidence that the nature of the thing admits. These facts are phaenomena of human nature, from which we may justly argue against any hypothesis, however generally received. But to argue from a hypothesis against facts, is contrary to the rules of true philosophy. (*CS*, 61)[1]

This is an apparent argument ad populum, and many of Reid's detractors have sought to discredit him on this basis. Reid is not, however, appealing to popular opinion but to the facts of our mental

---

1 All references to Reid in the text are from K. Lehrer and R. Beanblossom, eds., *Thomas Reid's Inquiry and Essays* (Indianapolis, IN: Bobbs-Merrill 1975). References to 'CS' are to *An Inquiry into the Human Mind on the Principles of Common Sense*, published in 1764, and references to 'IP' are to *Essays on the Intellectual Powers of Man*, published in 1785.

life. What we experience in this regard is the product 'of human nature' which we have 'by our constitution.' Thus, Reid replies to the sceptic, 'This belief, sir, is none of my manufacture; it came from the mint of Nature; ... I even took it upon trust, and without suspicion' (CS, 84). He notes that it would not be prudent to reject such beliefs, even if he could, and finally, he remarks that he has not been imposed upon by such beliefs. Indeed, he finds such 'instinctive beliefs' to be 'one of the best gifts of nature,' without which he would surely have perished by accident or remained in a state of nearly total ignorance.

Reid is aware that sceptics have admitted they cannot throw off such beliefs in practise, though they make war with them in speculation. He comments,

> It is a bold philosophy that rejects, without ceremony, principles which irresistibly govern the belief and the conduct of all mankind in the common concerns of life; and to which the philosopher himself must yield, after he imagines he hath confuted them. (*CS*, 9)

The critical point is that such beliefs are irresistible. Reid avers,

> ... that philosophy was never able to conquer that natural belief which men have in their senses; and that all their subtile reasonings against this belief were never able to persuade themselves. It appears, therefore, that the clear and distinct testimony of our senses carries irresistible conviction along with it to every man in his right judgment. (*IP*, 163)

This irresistible conviction is the sign of belief determined by the operation of some innate principle of our faculties. It is not merely the utility of such beliefs or even the universality of such beliefs that is basic to this reply to scepticism. On the contrary, the universality and irresistibility of such beliefs only testifies to their origin, to their being the result of original principles of our natural faculties.

Once it is thus shown that our beliefs are the result of such innate principles, Reid regards himself as having a decisive argument against the defenders of the ideal theory. For they were never so thorough in their scepticism as to bring into question the existence of impressions and ideas, and that is the Achilles heel of the ideal theory. Reid argues,

> ... that the belief of the existence of impressions and ideas, is as little supported by reason, as that of the existence of minds and bodies. No man ever

> did or could offer any reason for this belief ... . A thorough and consistent sceptic will never, therefore, yield this point. (*CS*, 57)

Thus, Descartes and the defenders of ideal theory assumed the fact of thought and therefore, of ideas. But, Reid asks, what testifies to that fact? Surely the only answer is our consciousness of our ideas, and so the faculty of consciousness is thus assumed to be trustworthy. Why should this faculty be assumed to be trustworthy and the other faculties, that of perception for example, be called into question?

Perhaps anticipating the reply that we cannot be deceived concerning the existence of our own ideas, Reid queries,

> Can any man prove that his consciousness may not deceive him? No man can; nor can we give a better reason for trusting to it, than that every man, while his mind is sound, is determined by the constitution of his nature, to give implicit belief to it. (*CS*, 4)

Moreover, the faculty of reason, elevated to a special position by the defenders of the ideal theory, who only admit the existence of what can be proven from our ideas by reason, occupies no special position in the quest for truth. Reid observes,

> Reason, says the sceptic, is the only judge of truth, and you ought to throw off every opinion and every belief that is not grounded on reason. Why, sir, should I believe the faculty of reason more than that of perception? — they both came out of the same shop, and were made by the same artist; if he puts one piece of false ware into my hands, what should hinder him from putting another? (*CS*, 85)

Thus, according to Reid, our faculties must all be regarded as trustworthy or all be rejected as untrustworthy, for we have no reason to regard one as more worthy of our trust than another.

To the thorough sceptic, Reid has no reply, but against the sceptical advocates of the ideal theory, Reid levels the charge of inconsistency. Reason as well as consciousness are trusted as a matter of course, but so are our other faculties. To require that all our other faculties be validated by reason when we have no grounds to regard reason as any more trustworthy than the other faculties is irrational. On the other hand, to place reason on the same level as our other faculties and thus to call its trustworthiness into question is to cause the ideal theory 'to split upon the rock' of its foundation. Thus, the theory must be either inconsistent or irrational.

In summary then, Reid argues against the ideal theory that it conflicts with facts and that it is either inconsistent or irrational. This, however, is not the only reason for rejecting the theory. Another reason for rejecting it is that 'we need not despair of a better.' The point is, of course, that Reid has a theory to offer that he considers superior to the ideal theory in that his is internally consistent and accords with facts. This is an important aspect of our interpretation of Reid, for Reid is much too readily represented as simply arguing that the ideal theory conflicts with common sense and therefore must be rejected. His argument is more complex, however, since he argues that common sense accords with the facts and consequently that a satisfactory theory of the human mind must accord with common sense. Moreover, Reid proposes such a theory, and it is to this theory of psychology that we now turn.

Reid's Theory of Perception

A central component of Reid's cognitive psychology is his theory of perception. According to Reid, physical impressions on the organs of sense cause sensations within the mind, which in turn give rise to the conception of qualities and objects of the external world and a conviction of their existence. He says that the sensations are *signs* of these qualities and objects and suggest the conception of them. For this notion of the *sign* relation, Reid is indebted to Berkeley, who said that sensations or 'ideas,' as he called them, were the language of nature or the language of God. Reid, however, does not treat the sensations as signs of other sensations to come, as Berkeley did, but as signs of the existence of qualities of external objects and of those objects themselves. Reid agrees with Berkeley, however, that the sensations are not at all similar to the qualities and objects they signify and suggest to us. Indeed, the sensations, which are activities or operations of the mind, are no more like what they signify than the words in a language are like what they signify or suggest to the mind.

This view of sensations as signs and of the subsequent analogy between perception and understanding language is thus fundamental. It is described by Reid as follows:

> There is a much greater similitude than is commonly imagined, between the testimony of nature given by our senses, and the testimony of men given by language. The credit we give to both is at first the effect of instinct only. When we grow up, and begin to reason about them, the credit given to human testimony is restrained and weakened, by the experience we have of deceit. But the credit given to the testimony of our senses, is established and confirmed by the uniformity and constancy of the laws of nature. (*CS*, 87)

We shall note later the implications of this passage for Reid's epistemology, especially the suggestion that the testimony of our senses is established and confirmed. But first we wish to clarify the psychological theory, for that is the basis of Reid's epistemology. To do this, we shall consider the manner in which he elaborates the analogy between language and perception.

Reid maintains that language and perception involve two different kinds of signs; one is natural and original, and the other is artificial and acquired by experience. To avoid confusion with modern terminology, we shall refer to the first sort of sign as *original*. These are signs we understand by virtue of some innate principle of our natural constitution. The second sort of signs are ones we understand as a result of experience and inductive reasoning, and they will be referred to as *acquired*. Acquired perception or language is inductively learned and consists of the acquired understanding of signs. According to Reid, there are perceptions and language processes that are acquired but which become so natural that they are easily mistaken for the original, but the distinction remains theoretically and empirically crucial. Just as there is no necessary connection between the signs of a conventional language and what they signify, so there is no necessary connection between sensations and what they signify. Some sensations are not utterly arbitrary signs, however, since they signify as a result of our natural constitution which, though it could have been otherwise, responds conceptually in uniform ways to sensation and sensory stimulation. These responses are the result of principles of our natural constitution.

The first sort of principle includes what Reid calls *particular* principles, which account for the particular conceptions of primary qualities, such as motion, depth, extension, hardness and so forth. In these cases, the sensations are original signs which immediately give rise to the conceptions of the qualities. Reid says of these signs,

> They pass through the mind instantaneously, and serve only to introduce the notion and belief of external things, which, by our constitution, are connected with them. They are natural signs, and the mind immediately passes to the thing signified, without making the least reflection upon the sign, or observing that there was any such thing. (*CS*, 47)

The operation of the mind by which it passes from the sensation to what it signifies is the result of the particular principle of our constitution which accounts for the particular conception arising from the sensation.

In the case of secondary qualities and their associated sensations, there is no particular principle which accounts for the conception that arises from the sensation. We are able to form only a *relative* notion of the quality as the unknown cause of the sensation. Reid says of such a quality,

> We conceive it only as that which occasions such a sensation, and therefore cannot reflect upon it without thinking of the sensation which it occasions: we have no other mark whereby to distinguish it. (*IP*, 185)

Instead of a particular principle yielding a clear and distinct conception, as in the case of primary qualities, there is only a *general* principle of our constitution. This *inductive principle* accounts for our conception of secondary qualities, smells, tastes, sounds, colors, and so forth, as whatever is the cause of the associated sensation. Reid says,

> ... That effects of the same kind must have the same cause; for *effects* and *causes*, in the operations of nature, mean nothing but signs and the things signified by them. (*CS*, 101)

The operation of such a principle in yielding the conception of secondary qualities does not involve reasoning of any sort. The general principle yields a conception of the quality as the cause of the sensation without reflection or argumentation. These conceptions of secondary qualities, in that they involve the operation of the inductive principle, are acquired and not original. We learn to conceive of these qualities through the operation of the inductive principle, which gives rise to the belief that sensations of the same kind have the same cause whatever it may be. This conception of a cause is relative to the sensation and thus differs from the clear and distinct conception of a primary quality.

It is interesting to notice that, while Reid rejects the theory of Locke concerning primary and secondary qualities, he preserves the distinction. Reid rejects the view that secondary qualities are mental entities such as ideas or sensations, and he also rejects the view that primary qualities resemble such entities. Sensations are mental operations and do not resemble the qualities of external material things. The difference between primary and secondary qualities is in terms of our manner of conception of them. Specifically, our conception of a primary quality is innate in the sense that it arises immediately from the sensation according to a particular principle of our constitution. Our conception of a secondary quality, on the other hand, is mediated by a general principle of learning, the inductive principle, and is merely the conception of an unknown cause of our sensation. This aspect of Reid's thought is important for it illustrates his commitment to restricting hypotheses to the facts. Reid seeks to attribute as little to our natural constitution, to innate principles, as is required by the facts. He thinks that the conception we have of primary qualities could not be learned inductively, because we can inductively learn only of some unknown cause of a sensation. He notes that, as a matter of fact, our conception is richer, clearer and more distinct, as he puts it, than could be obtained by induction. He concludes that such conceptions arise from particular principles of our constitution in response to sensations. No learning is required. But our conceptions of secondary qualities are not so rich, not clear and distinct, as a matter of fact, and therefore, could be learned inductively. It is worth noting that there is some empirical evidence that Reid was right about this matter.[2]

---

2 Cf. K. Allan, 'Classifiers,' *Language*, 53 (1977) 285-311, esp. 298

Finally, to complete our sketch of Reid's theory of perception, we note that, in addition to the conception of qualities and objects, there is the 'immediate and irresistible' belief in their existence which is the result of a further general principle of the perceptual faculty. Reid says,

> I know this also, that the perception of an object implies both a conception of its form, and a belief of its present existence. I know, moreover, that this belief is not the effect of argumentation and reasoning; it is the immediate effect of my constitution. (*CS*, 84)

The general principle, which we shall call the *principle of perceptual reality*, is 'That those things do really exist which we distinctly perceive by our senses, and are what we perceive them to be' (*IP*, 272). By this general principle, 'when the perception is in any degree clear and steady, there remains no doubt of it's reality' (*IP*, 161). Perception is a mental operation beginning with the interpretation of sensory signs according to the particular or general principles of our constitution which yield conceptions. When those conceptions are 'clear and steady,' the final stage of the perception, a conviction that what we conceive exists and is what we conceive it to be, immediately arises without reasoning or argumentation.

It can also be the case with some complex perceptions that reasoning plays a role, as when I hear a sound and *conclude* that it is the sound of some object that I remember to be caused by some object from past experience. This sort of reasoning may appeal to belief in the inductive principle as a premise for drawing a conclusion. When the inductive principle is used in this way in reasoning, the principle functions in a quite different manner from when it immediately produces conviction without reasoning. The more typical case of perception is one in which no appeal to belief in the inductive principle is made, no reasoning occurs, and the principle gives rise to conviction without itself becoming the object of belief or reflection. Indeed, when reasoning is involved in producing conviction, the conviction is perhaps best described as the product of reason, but people do speak of hearing or perceiving in such cases. These are complex convictions in which perception as well as reason plays a role, and though they are not pure cases of perception, they may without abuse of language be called complex perceptions.

Keith Lehrer and John-Christian Smith

Reid's Theory of Language

This sketch of the functioning of the perceptual faculty is taken by Reid to be directly analogous to that of the language faculty. He remarks,

> The signs by which objects are presented to us in perception, are the language of Nature to man; and as, in many respects, it hath great affinity with the language of man to man, so particularly in this, that both are partly natural and original, partly acquired by custom. Our original or natural perceptions are analogous to the [original] language of man to man ... and our acquired perceptions are analogous to [acquired] language, which, in our mother tongue, is got very much in the same manner with our acquired perceptions ... (*CS*, 88)

Reid further concludes,

> In the testimony of Nature given by the senses, as well as in human testimony given by language, things are signified to us by signs; and in one as well as the other, the mind, either by original principles or by custom, passes from the sign to the conception and belief of the things signified. (*CS*, 90)

Thus, the parallel between the perceptual faculty and the language faculty includes the functioning of particular principles and general principles in both faculties which produce conception and conviction in response to signs.

Reid maintains that the 'natural signs' of our original language, the language we understand innately, are 'features of the face, gestures of the body, and modulations of the voice' (*CS*, 90). There is a natural connection between these phenomena and particular thoughts and dispositions of the mind. The particular principles of the language faculty produce conceptions of the thoughts and dispositions signified by these phenomena. The parallel to primary qualities in the case of perception is clear. Reid notes,

> Our original perceptions, as well as the [original] language of human features and gestures, must be resolved into particular principles of the human constitution. Thus, it is be one particular principle of our constitution that certain features express anger; and, by another particular principle, that certain features express benevolence. (*CS*, 91-2)

The connection between the sign in original language and the thing signified is determined by the 'natural knowledge,' 'previous to experience,' inherent in the particular principles of the faculty (*CS*, 41,90). The interpretation of these signs according to such principles occurs by our nature and does not involve reasoning or custom.

The analogy extends to the operation of general principles by means of which we understand the signs of conventional or acquired language. Reid notes that 'our acquired perceptions, and the information we receive by means of [acquired] language, must be resolved into general principles of the human constitution' (*CS*, 92). The perceptual signs in acquired language are articulate sounds, 'whose connection with the things signified by them is established by the will of men' and discovered by experience with the aid of the original language (*CS*, 91). As in the perception of secondary qualities (and more complex perceptions), the discovery proceeds according to a general principle. This is the *principle of credulity* which is that 'our fellow creatures will use the same signs in language, when they have the same sentiments' (*CS*, 93). Reid takes this to be 'an original principle of the human constitution, without which we should be incapable of language, and consequently incapable of instruction' (*CS*, 93).

The principle of credulity of the language faculty plays a parallel role to the inductive principle of the faculty of perception in the understanding of signs beyond those that are natural or original. Moreover, there is even an analogy between our understanding of secondary qualities and our understanding of individual words in a language. Reid (*CS*, 92), suggests that the child, learning to imitate articulate sounds, learns in such a way that the 'sentiment' expressed by the sound of another is conceived by the child as whatever is the cause of the sound, according to the principle that like effects will be produced from the same cause.

As a final point of similarity, beliefs arise from the principle of credulity just as they do from the principle of induction. Reid notes this similarity between inductive and, what we might call credulous beliefs, though he is quick to point out that the deceptions that often disappoint us when our beliefs are produced by the principle of credulity, as contrasted with those produced by the inductive principle, are due to the character of man differing from Nature (*CS*, 102). Nevertheless, the principle of credulity is not by any means useless as a guide to truth because, according to Reid, there is an instinctual 'propensity to speak truth and to use the signs of language so as to convey our real sentiments' (*CS*, 94).

This propensity is a product of a general principle of the language faculty, the *principle of veracity*. For Reid, this is no mere inclination but rather, 'a powerful operation' and 'the natural issue of the mind' (*CS*, 94). He finds,

> ... that truth is always at the door of my lips, and goes forth spontaneously, if not held back. It requires neither good nor bad intentions to bring it forth, but only that I be artless and undesigning ... we speak truth by instinct – and this instinct is the principle I have been explaining. (*CS*, 94)

The principle of veracity thus plays an analogous role to the principle of perceptual reality, for by each of these principles the conceptions and beliefs of a faculty are taken as a guide to truth. As Reid remarks of the signs produced by others, in comparision to the signs produced by our senses,

> ... so remarkable is the analogy between these two, and the analogy between the principles of the mind which are subservient to the one and those which are subservient to the other, that, without further apology, we shall consider them together. (*CS*, 90)

In summary, then, we find that Reid has a cognitive information processing theory of how we understand the signs others produce as well as the signs produced by our own senses. This modern and cogent account is unified in terms of the principles that explain the operations of the mind in interpreting signs of various sorts. This interpretation proceeds at the simplest level in terms of particular principles according to which particular signs are interpreted, for example, when we take some sign as a sign of motion or anger. Other more general principles allow us to learn, through experience, the meaning of signs which we do not understand innately, for example, those pertaining to secondary qualities or individual words. These general principles function to form conception and belief at first without reasoning, and we may be said to instantiate or exemplify these principles, as well as the particular principles, rather than reasoning from them. Finally, however, reason intercedes, and we reason from these principles as premises to arrive at yet further knowledge and conviction.

We think that it is most important to notice that this theory of cognitive psychology has a crucial characteristic derived from Reid's commitment to the methodology of Bacon, to wit, the frugality of the hypotheses concerning what is to be innately attributed to the human constitution. Unlike traditional philosophers such as Kant who attribute an architectonic structure to the mind, Reid asks what minimal attribution will account for the facts. Unlike some modern cognitive psychologists, Reid refuses to attribute a complex conceptual system to the mind. In other ways, however, his model bears a striking similarity to modern proposals concerning the modularity of mind.[3] Let us now turn to an account of the relation between Reid's psychology and his epistemology.

Reid's Epistemology

The general statement of Reid's epistemology is simple enough, but it conceals an internal complexity. Reid says that the principles of our constitution are *first principles* of epistemology. Thus, the evidence of our senses, like the evidence of testimony, is the consequence of first principles. In Reid's early work he says,

> To reason against any of these kinds of evidence, is absurd; nay, to reason for them is absurd. They are first principles; and such fall not within the province of reason, but of common sense. (*CS*, 19)

This idea is repeated in his later work, but with a minor modification:

> As there are words common to philosophers and to the vulgar, which need no explication, so there are principles common to both, which need no proof, and which do not admit of direct proof... (*IP*, 151)

3 Cf., e.g., J.A. Fodor, *The Modularity of Mind*, A Bradford Book (Cambridge, MA: The MIT Press 1983)

The important qualification is contained in the word 'direct.' Reid observes that

> ...although it is contrary to the nature of first principles to admit of direct or *apodictical* proof; yet there are certain ways of reasoning even about them, by which those that are just and solid may be confirmed, and those that are false may be detected. (*IP*, 261)

Such reasoning need not constitute an argument for the truth of first principles or the beliefs to which they give rise but only an argument to show that the beliefs do, in fact, arise from the operation of a first principle of our faculties.

One sort of argument of this kind arises from consensus or agreement among mankind, except perhaps lunatics and philosophers, for example, concerning the existence of the material world. This shows, Reid argues, that the belief in question arises from some innate principle. He suggests that one way in which to discover such consensus is to consider the languages of the world to ascertain what common beliefs are embodied within them, such as, for example, that thoughts are always the thoughts of a thinking subject and qualities are always the qualities of an object that has them. This sort of reasoning is, however, reasoning intended to show that some belief is the product of an innate principle of our constitution; it is not a proof of the truth of the belief. Moreover, Reid admits that we may be mistaken in what we take to be a first principle and that we must be ready to hear what may be pleaded to the contrary.

From the assumption that some principle is an innate principle of our constitution, Reid infers as a first principle of epistemology that the beliefs arising from it are ones for which we have evidence or which are evident. He says,

> We give the name of evidence to whatever is a ground of belief. (*IP*, 199)

He then goes on to say, after noting that he cannot find any common nature to which all kinds of evidence may be reduced, that

> They seem to me to agree only in this, that they are all fitted by Nature to produce belief in the human mind, some of them in the highest degree,

> which we call certainty, others in various degrees according to circumstances. (*IP*, 201)

Reid holds that the first principles not only produce beliefs but supply the grounds of those beliefs at the same time. As we have noted above, Reid does not regard our faculties as infallible guides to truth. Not even the faculty of consciousness is infallible. But that leaves us with an obvious problem. If our faculties are not infallible, then what reason do we have to believe that they are a trustworthy guide to truth and are not fallacious? The answer is straightforward: it is a first principle. Reid contends that in addition to first principles concerning perception and our other faculties,

> Another principle is — *That the natural faculties, by which we distinguish truth from error, are not fallacious*. If any man should demand a proof of this, it is impossible to satisfy him. ... because, to judge of demonstration, a man must trust his faculties, and take for granted the very thing in question. (*IP*, 275)

These remarks are crucial for an understanding of Reid's epistemology. They tell us why we cannot give a proof of a first principle and explain how we may nevertheless reason in a certain way regarding them and thus confirm them. Moreover, they show that Reid's theory is a sophisticated combination of a foundation theory of knowledge with reliablism and a coherence theory.

It is useful to notice first the degree to which Reid, perhaps influenced by his interest in Aristotle, insists that there must be first principles. The reason why these do not admit of proof is clear. Any attempt to prove a first principle leads to a circle and begs the question. It is interesting to notice what fundamental importance Reid attaches to the precept that arguing in a circle proves nothing. He lists it under logical axioms.

> There are *logical* axioms: such as, ... *That every proposition is either true or false: That no proposition can be both true and false at the same time: That reasoning in a circle proves nothing.* (*IP*, 285)

Thus, it is clear why we can give no proof of first principles, because to do so would be to argue in a circle and to prove nothing.

Moreover, it is clear that these first principles provide us with the premises for further reasoning. To this extent, Reid is a typical foundation theorist arguing that we must have first principles which give us immediate knowledge from which all other knowledge is derived. He is, however, a somewhat unusual foundation theorist in that he argues that our faculties which yield beliefs according to first principles are not infallible, though it is first principle that these faculties are not fallacious. As we noted above, in his early work, Reid says of the testimony of our senses in comparison to that of men,

> But the credit given to the testimony of our senses, is established and confirmed by the uniformity and constancy of the laws of nature. (*CS*, 87)

We noted also that this view is reiterated in the later work, as well, when he says that we can reason about first principles, so that those that are just and solid may be confirmed and those that are false detected.

Here, however, it seems as though Reid has fallen into inconsistency. If we can reason concerning first principles and confirm that some principles are just and solid, why is this not a proof of the veracity of these principles? Reid says,

> Every kind of reasoning for the veracity of our faculties amounts to no more than taking their own testimony for their veracity; and this we must do implicitly... . (*IP*, 276)

This passage, in the words, 'and this we must do implicitly,' brings us to a solution. We recall that Reid says that it is a first principle that our faculties are not fallacious. Further, Reid says in reply to Hume that we must regard all of our faculties as trustworthy or none. Given that it is a first principle that our faculties are not fallacious, we can see that there is a connection between first principles. If it is a first principle that our faculties are not fallacious, then the beliefs that arise from those principles enable us to discover laws of nature by principles of the faculty of perception and the inductive principle. But these laws of nature include the laws of *our* nature, and therefore, we may discover that the testimony of our faculties, as contrasted with the testimony of men on some occasions, is a trustworthy guide to truth.

What are to make of this reasoning? Clearly, according to Reid it is no proof of the trustworthiness of the faculty, for it assumes the trustworthiness of the faculties as a point of departure. However, as Reid notes in his early refutation of the ideal theory, to assume that the testimony of one faculty only is trustworthy is to fall into inconsistency, but he adds, to accept the testimony of all presupposes 'there must, therefore, be some order and consistency in the human faculties' (*CS*, 53). In the later work, he puts the matter even more strongly. There he affirms that to deny a first principle will lead to a proof ad absurdum of the error. The reason is,

> There is hardly any proposition, especially of those that may claim the character of first principles, that stands alone and unconnected. It draws many others along with it in a chain that cannot be broken. He that takes it up must bear the burden of all its consequences; and, if that is too heavy for him to bear, he must not pretend to take it up. (*IP*, 261)

Thus, the system of first principles and their consequences must yield a coherent system, and, therefore, anyone who denies a first principle is subject to reduction to absurdity. One first principle tells us that our faculties are not fallacious, and the first principles of our faculties enable us to discover those laws of nature which confirm that our faculties and their first principles are trustworthy. This is not a *direct* proof, for, as Reid notes, to reason in this way is to reason in a circle. But first principles do admit of *indirect* proof *ad absurdum* because the system of first principles yields a system of propositions connected in a chain that cannot be broken without falling into absurdity. The indirect proof of the trustworthiness of our faculties is a consequence of the coherence of the system.

Summary

Reid's analogy between the faculty of perception and the faculty of language articulates a theory of cognition as information processing of natural signs in terms of innate principles. These principles are first principles in the sense of being innate principles that originate our conceptions and in the sense of being principles that originate evidence for the beliefs that they produce. The first principles give rise to our conceptions and convictions. They also give rise to convictions that are evident. The connection between the innateness of the principles and the evidence of the beliefs they produce is effected by what is itself a first principle, to wit, that our faculties are reliable and not fallacious as a guide to obtaining truth and avoiding error. The analogy between the testimony of others and the testimony of our senses illustrates the point. When we are convinced by the testimony of others, we must regard their testimony as trustworthy and not fallacious, that is, as evidence of truth. By analogy when we are convinced by the testimony of our senses or the testimony of any other faculty of our nature, we must regard this testimony as trustworthy and not fallacious, that is, as evidence of truth. Reid's theory of the first principles of our faculties, which is the foundation of his cognitive psychology, includes as a first principle that those faculties are trustworthy, if fallible, guides to truth and the avoidance of error. To suppose that first principles are not so trustworthy is, given our natural constitution, to fall victim to incoherence and inconsistency. Common sense is psychologically coherent, scepticism is not.[4]

Received May, 1983

---

4 The senior author gratefully acknowledges support of this research by a grant from the National Science Foundation.

CANADIAN JOURNAL OF PHILOSOPHY
Supplementary Volume 11

*Searle on Programs and Intentionality**

RICHARD SHARVY
2447 Kincaif Street
Eugene, OR 97405
U.S.A.

... it is possible for a man to write a piece correctly by chance or at the prompting of another: but he will be literate only if he produces a piece of writing in a literate way, and that means doing it in accordance with the skill of literate composition which he has in himself.

Aristotle, *Nicomachean Ethics* II 4 1105a23-35

* I thank Daniel Dennett, Edward Erwin, Dale Jamieson, Cristelle Leaf, William G. Lycan, Alice Perrin, and Morton Winston for their good conversation and correspondence on many of these problems. A version of this paper was read to the Florida Philosophical Association in November 1981.

Richard Sharvy

> A man blind from birth might produce syllogisms about colours, but he is reasoning only about names to which nothing in his mind corresponds.
> *Physics* II 1 193a7-9

John Searle has published an exciting discussion of the relations between computer programs and intentionality. His Chinese Room Example shows a principle of non-sufficiency, namely that

NAS: instantiating a computer program is not always by itself a sufficient condition of intentionality.

From this, Searle infers that 'The *explanation* of how the brain produces intentionality cannot be that it does it *by* instantiating a computer program' (417, my italics). And from this, Searle concludes that programs produced by workers in artificial intelligence can never provide an adequate theory of any intentionality.

Searle's aim is to dispute certain strong claims from the field of AI: (1) that a particular computing machine literally understands English, (2) that it has this intentional attribute in virtue of the program it is running, and (3) that the structure of that program therefore reveals something about how the soul understands English.

Now it seems that many of Searle's critics have not understood his aim. He has been criticised as if he had been arguing that 'computers cannot think.' No such conclusion is his goal at all. In fact he states that '*only* a machine could think, and indeed only very special kinds of machines, namely brains and machines that had the same causal powers as brains' (424).

However, there are problems with Searle's arguments. For one thing, it is not completely clear what 'causal properties of the brain' he has in mind. For another, there is an ambiguity in his phrase 'instantiate a computer program.' The ambiguity is the same as that in 'follow a rule' and 'obey a law.' Strong sense: a man, such as Searle himself in his thought-experiment, might *literally follow* a rule or a set of instructions, in that he intentionally acts in accordance with such instructions, which he understands and is aware of. Weak sense: a group of billiard balls might *exhibit a regularity* expressed by e.g., the law of conservation of momentum, and in that sense they could be said to obey the law of conservation of momentum.

The question then is which sense of 'instantiating' is meant in Searle's claim that the brain does not produce intentionality by instantiating a program. More generally, in which sense do computing machines instantiate programs? I believe that one problem in discussing minds (souls, actually) and machines has been a failure to take this distinction seriously, and to assume that there is something 'in between' these two sorts of instantiating – a sort of 'unconscious but literal' following of rules.

Related to this problem is a lack of clarity on Searle's part about what does and does not follow from NAS (which he does undeniably establish). I will point out the importance of the words 'by itself' in NAS, as well as problems that would be involved in trying to show something about *necessary* conditions for having various intentionalities. I will also note that Searle's own version of NAS, which has 'never' where I have 'not always,' is too strong and does not follow from his example.

I. The Example and Theorem

Searle's argument has three parts: (1) the Chinese Room Example, (2) a conclusion that seems to follow from it, which I shall call the Chinese Room Theorem, and (3) the supposed implications of the Theorem. Here is the Chinese Room Example: imagine that John R. Searle is locked in a room, and that he has a pack of cards with Chinese characters printed on them and an instruction book. The instructions in the book, an AI program, specify which cards are to be pushed out of the room through a slot, as a function of cards that are going to be pushed in. Then, some cards with Chinese characters are pushed in, and Searle follows the instructions in the book and pushes some cards out. From outside the room then, it seems that the man in the room understands Chinese. For the cards that were pushed in tell a story in Chinese about restaurants, and then ask questions in Chinese about the story, and the cards that come out give sensible and grammatical replies in Chinese. But the man in the room, Searle himself, in fact does not understand Chinese. Thus, *S* simulates being in state *C* by following an algorithm, but *S* is not in state *C*. That is the Chinese Room Example.

I would revise Searle's example slightly, by supposing that the instruction book states everything in terms of positive integers written on the backs of the cards, so that he does not need to pay any attention to the Chinese characters on the front. This makes it clearer that even if Searle 'internalizes' the rule book, he still has not learned Chinese. It is consistent with the ways that symbols are represented within a computer, and it serves to remind us of the Skolem-Löwenheim theorem and of the opacity of representation and intentionality.

Douglas Hofstadter complained that Searle ignores the fact that he would be very, very slow in producing his responses — much slower than a computer or a speaker of Chinese (433). But suppose that Searle is a calculating prodigy and computes his responses very quickly. (Remember, everything is represented as arithmetic.) Is this possible? Of course it is.

In fact, suppose that for any sequence of cards pushed into the room, the AI program in question produces the same response that a real Chinese speaker would produce. Then aren't real speakers of Chinese just such calculating prodigies? (Or, at any rate, doesn't AI dogma claim that they are?)

Calculating prodigies generally use a variety of tricks. In this case, a real Chinese speaker locked in the room might compute the complicated numerical function by interpreting the sequences of positive integers coming into the room as stories and questions in Chinese about restaurants. Searle himself might develop a different trick.

The Chinese Room Example challenges the claims by AI enthusiasts that a computer responding in English to English inputs actually understands English, and does so by executing a program — for we see that an entity might follow an algorithm and simulate having an intentional attribute *C*, without actually having that intentional attribute *C*. Hence, the Chinese Room Theorem:

CRT: There do not exist a program, a computer, and an intentional attribute such that the computer can come to have the attribute *just by* instantiating the program.

For just pick a person who lacks the attribute, and have him follow the program, on the model of Searle in his room.[1] The person will still lack the intentionality; thus, the power to produce that intentionality is not in the program. At least the power to produce that intentionality *in humans* is not in that program. CRT follows if we can infer that since this is true of humans, it is also true of computers. Is there some doctrine that strong AI is committed to that would force its defenders to allow this inference?

Now Searle certainly does not claim that instantiating a program is sufficient for *lacking* any particular intentionality. If *I* were locked in the Chinese Room following that algorithm, I would not understand Chinese *by* following the algorithm, but I do understand Chinese, and I would continue to do so while following the algorithm. Following the algorithm does not cause me to stop knowing Chinese. This leaves it open that a computer might understand English or Chinese. The significance of the Theorem is supposed to be that even if a computer does understand Chinese, its program does not *explain* how it does this; however, I shall argue that the Chinese Room Theorem has no such implications.

II. What Programs and Computers Do

The old distinction mentioned above (between intentionally following a rule and merely behaving in accordance with one) has application here, because computers do not literally execute programs! Searle, in the room, is executing instructions, but computers just do not do any such thing.

Many people believe that computers do execute instructions. They believe this because the popular press says so, because computer science textbooks say so, and because the experience of apparently

---

1 This will not work if the state in question is just plain thinking. If I merely claim that a certain program, running on a computer, produces thought, there is no Chinese Room Example to refute this, since the man in the room has to think to literally follow the program.

giving instructions to a computer, which it then apparently executes, is a quite common one.

A minor bit of sophistication appears in computer science textbooks. Typically, it is explained that a program that you write in a programming language, such as Fortran or Algol, has to be translated into another language, a machine language, that the computer can 'understand.' Then, so the explanation goes, the computer will execute those machine-language instructions (after also including needed subroutines, etc.). But the computer user generally does not need to worry about this, because the computer itself will do that job of translating.

So, when you enter a sequence of instructions such as

```
DO (N=1,100)
PRINT N, 'I WILL NOT PUSH IN LINE'
FIN
```

the computer does not execute *those* instructions. It translates them into a sequence of perhaps three times as many machine instructions, and then, supposedly, it executes those.

How? Obviously, nothing worth mentioning has been explained yet. The above 'explanation' is metaphorical and question-begging. It leaves us still in the dark about the details of the process by which the computer supposedly reads an instruction and then carries it out. That this explanation is worthless and incoherent seems to have gone unnoticed.

The solution to this problem is that computers just do not do any such thing. They do not execute instructions, and they do not execute sequences of instructions (i.e., programs). This is so whether the instructions are in a quasi-natural algorithmic programming language or in a so-called machine language. (For an example of this confusion, see Smythe's reply, p. 448, col. 2.) Now computers do *appear* to execute instructions, and we can *represent* their behaviour as that of executing a set of instructions. But literally they do no such thing.

Let me elaborate. Many years ago my father and I built a little machine for solving syllogisms. The front of the machine had two wheels and a row of lights. Wheel 1 could be turned to any one of several positions, representing forms in '*A*' and '*B*,' such as 'all *A* is *B*,' 'some *B* is not *A*'; wheel 2 was similar, except that its positions represented forms in '*B*' and '*C*.' The lights were labeled with forms in '*A*' and '*C*,' and one was labeled 'no conclusion.' Setting the wheels to two premises resulted in the appropriate light going on.

How? Was the machine following instructions? No. The back was a maze of wires, and the principles involved were the elementary ones of series and parallel circuits.

One could build a machine for playing tic-tac-toe (noughts and crosses) or chess in just the same way. First, draw a wiring diagram, and then get out your soldering gun and some wire. It is in fact quite reasonable to imagine building a tic-tac-toe machine this way. However, the wiring diagram for a decent chess-playing machine would be so complicated that no mere human would be able to draw it in the first place.

This is where programs enter. A task such as deciding a chess move or calculating a cosine is described as a sequence of discrete steps. Suppose then that we had a device that could automatically turn this description into wiring. Then we would have a much easier job of building a chess machine: we would write a program and feed it to this device, and it would build the machine. Of course the program has to be written in a formalized language and represented in a way that will cause physical action to take place. That is easy to arrange – represent it by holes punched on paper tape, like a player piano roll.

Now we have (a) our algorithm, (b) its representation as a sequence of holes punched on tape, (c) the machine that the tape is fed to, and (d) the machine that is then constructed as a result. The machine and wiring that result might be made small – burned into a silicon chip, perhaps. The resulting machine is identical in kind with one built directly from a wiring diagram. Neither executes programs. Neither contains instructions. In fact this is exactly how chess-playing microcomputers are made.

Programs then have two quite distinct uses: (1) to build complex machines, and (2) to represent complex behaviour. The machines that are built with them do not themselves execute instructions. In use (2), as a representation of what a machine or a person is doing, a program is often easy for humans to use and understand. But for this representational use, the program does not need to be written in a formal programming language at all – a flow chart or informally stated algorithm will do. Now although such an algorithm can be a useful representation of what a machine is doing, computers do not literally execute programs. Searle, locked in the room, is literally following an algorithm, but this is a very special case. Most of the time, neither people nor machines are literally following programs.

I have not said that it is *impossible* for a computer to literally follow instructions. If a computer were built with the 'causal powers of the brain,' then possibly it could understand English and thus literally follow instructions written in English. And then, we could give it Searle's book of instructions and lock it in a room with that book and the cards with the Chinese characters... . It would understand English, but it would still not understand Chinese!

As another example of programs as representations, consider a system of self-service elevators in a large hotel. By sufficient playing with the system, we could produce a written program that would exactly represent the behaviour of the system. ('Send nearest elevator to answer call unless going in opposite direction, in which case... unless... etc.') But even if this sequence of instructions (i.e., this program) is a perfect representation of the elevator system's behaviour, it does not follow that the system is executing any instructions at all. (Newer elevator systems have parts of their wiring actually generated via programs, i.e., they are controlled by microcomputers, but this is clearly irrelevant.)

In which sense do actual computing machines 'instantiate' or follow or execute programs? Only in the weak sense: they exhibit regularities which can be expressed by algorithms written in formalized programming languages. In which sense does Searle himself in his thought-experiment instantiate a program? In the strong sense: he literally follows a sequence of instructions. The strong sense implies the weak, so Searle in the room also instantiates the algorithm in the weak sense – his behaviour accords with it.

Art is representation aimed at beauty. Science is representation aimed at explanation. To describe a thermostat or a player piano or a computer as following instructions might be pretty and useful, but it is not a good explanation of anything, and therefore it is not good science. It is a gross confusion to say that a hole in a certain place in a piece of paper is a player-piano-language instructing meaning 'hit middle C.' There just is no player piano language, and there just is no machine language for any computer. A player piano does not follow instructions. Neither does an elevator system or a computer. A program is a *representation of* what such machines are doing.

III. Some Remarks about Representation

It is easy to confuse representing with being. Is this dot on the map Wellington, New Zealand? Of course not — the dot is much too small. Is the number two the set {0, {0} }? Of course not — the set has two members, and the number two does not. Of course that set might be used to *represent* the number two. Representation is one of the most important notions in the history of philosophy, mathematics, and in the sciences and arts generally.[2]

J.L. Synge has a nice name for the error of mistaking a representation of something for the real thing. Synge calls this the *Pygmalion Syndrome,* after the mythological king who fell in love with a statue. Describing a computer as executing instructions is an example. So is thinking that the number two could really be {0, {0} }.

Pygmalion Syndrome is obviously epidemic among workers in the field of so-called artificial intelligence. As Searle points out, nobody would confuse a computer simulation of a storm with a real storm, but computer simulations of intelligence are often described as intelligent. So-called artificial intelligence is probably only *simulated* or *imitation* intelligence rather than genuine artificial intelligence.[3]

---

2 Exercise: read *Republic* VI 509d-511e; then rewrite the last chapter of *Word and Object,* putting 'represent by' for 'identify with' throughout. Possibly the only real disagreement between Quine and Plato is simply over whether our understanding of abstract ideals is clearer or muddier than our understanding of symbols for them.

3 Being artificial implies being actual: AI can get you just as pregnant as the natural sort (AI = artificial insemination). A simulated insemination of you might be run on a computer, but you would not need to worry about it any

The mindless reply to Searle by Douglas Hofstadter is a good example of Pygmalion Syndrome gone wild. Hofstadter takes the entire question to be one involving merely a conflict of religious dogma. He then tells us that he specifically counts himself among those who 'find in reductionism the ultimate religion' (434). Reductionism, at its worst, is the belief that if you have constructed a representation of something (e.g., points and lines) in terms of something else (e.g., classes, real numbers, and ordered pairs), then the something actually is the something else. This is obviously just more Pygmalion Syndrome.

And intelligence is one thing, consciousness another. Attributing intelligence to something, person or machine, seems independent of attributing consciousness or intentionality to it. I am even willing to be totally behaviouristic about intelligence – but not about intentional states, such as understanding Chinese.

In any event, Searle is not presenting any argument about the limits of *simulated* intelligence. There may be programs that pass the Turing test. If not, wait until next year.

Searle's Chinese Room Example does establish without doubt that the Turing test is invalid. But the Turing test should not be thought of as a test of *intelligence* in the first place. If we want a test of intelligence, we need not look far. We already have standard intelligence tests, taken by thousands of high school students every year. I suggest then this challenge to AI: write a program that will consistently get decent scores on these standardized tests. (No complaints about cultural bias, please!)

---

more than you need to worry about someone's throwing darts at your photograph.

Being actual is not quite the same as being real; if someone dyes his grey hair black, the actual colour is then black, but the real colour is grey; 'real' can mean 'original'. 'Artificial' can sometimes seem to mean 'imitation', as in 'artificial flowers', but I find this a bit of a misnomer. An imitation hand merely has to look like a natural hand, but an artificial hand must do the work of a natural hand, even if it does not look like one. If the only work required of flowers is to look flowery, then that would explain why imitation ones are called artificial. A plastic imitation tree could be an artificial Christmas tree, but it could not be an artificial apple tree, although it might be an imitation apple tree.

IV. Programs as Theories

But what of the Chinese Room Theorem? The Chinese Room Example shows that instantiating (in the strong sense of literally following) a set of instructions is not *always by itself* sufficient for any intentionality. Does it follow that for anything that does have a particular intentionality *C*, such as an understanding of Chinese, it does not have it *by* following any program or algorithm? Certainly not. Turning the key in my ignition switch is not *by itself* sufficient for starting my car, as I am occasionally reminded by a dead battery. Does it follow that I never start my car *by* turning the key? Of course not. When other necessary conditions are satisfied, I do start my car by turning the key.

It is for this reason that I have put the word 'just' in my version of the Chinese Room Theorem. Turning a key is not *by itself* sufficient for starting my car; therefore, the explanation of my car's starting is not *just* that I turn a key. But so what? My turning the key is still an important *part* of the explanation of my car's starting. So just what is the significance of the Chinese Room Theorem? Notice that it leaves wide open the possibility that literally following a computer program could still be an important *part* of the explanation of intentionalities. What Searle has shown is that instantiating a program cannot always be the *whole* story. This may not seem to be much – but remember, his target is only the excesses of what he calls 'strong AI.'

Some of the locutions used by Searle are worth a comment. The following are equivalent: *A* is not by itself a sufficient condition for *B*; *A* is not always a sufficient condition for *B*; *A* is not a sufficient condition for *B* unless *C* (for some particular *C*); *A* is a sufficient condition for *B* only if *C*; *A* is at most a *proper part* of the explanation of *B*; *A* is not the whole of the explanation of *B*. And then there is a second group of locutions, distinct from these, but equivalent to each other: *A* is not by itself a necessary condition for *B*: *A* is not always a necessary condition for *B*; *A* is not a necessary condition for *B* unless *D* (for some particular *D*); *A* is a necessary condition for *B* only if *D*; *A* is not necessary to explain *B*; *A* is not the only possible explanation of *B*.

It is true that for every program *P* and every intentional state *C*, literally following (strong sense) program *P* is not enough to guarantee being in state *C*, since a man in a room could follow the program without being in the state. From this, and the fact that literally following (strong sense) a program *P is* sufficient for instantiating *P* in the weak sense, it does follow that instantiating (weak sense) a program *P* is not enough to guarantee being in *C* either. And *of course* nothing can have *C* (e.g., an understanding of Chinese) *by, through,* or *in virtue of* exhibiting the regularity represented by a program.

Consider this parallel to Searle's argument. A quadrilateral (a man in a room) can be equi-angular (can instantiate a program *P*) without being equilateral (without understanding Chinese); therefore, being equi-angular is 'not always by itself sufficient' for being equilateral. But it just does not follow that being equi-angular is *never* sufficient for being equilateral. For *triangles,* being equi-angular is sufficient for being equilateral. What is true of quadrilaterals (i.e., that being equi-angular is not by itself sufficient for being equilateral) is not true of triangles.

Now let us put 'computer' or 'brain' in place of 'triangle' in this argument. We see that the Chinese Room Example shows NAS, but does not generalize to the Chinese Room Theorem. NAS is fairly weak; it says that instantiating a program is *not always* by itself sufficient. Searle's own version said that instantiating a program is *never* by itself sufficient for intentionality. But that does not follow from the Chinese Room Example. (For further discussion of this point see Sharvy 1983.)

Consider the complex property of *being such that instantiating an AI program that simulates an understanding of Chinese is not by itself sufficient for actually understanding Chinese.* Humans have this property, as the Chinese Room Example demonstrates. Then if all computers were humans, all computers would have it also, and we could derive the general Chinese Room Theorem. But even strong AI does not hold that all computers are humans. Searle needs to give us a precisely formulated dogma of strong AI that he can use against AI by showing that the dogma allows the inference from his example to the general theorem.

It is interesting that Searle does not attempt to show *converse* examples. Why hasn't he provided us with a man who understands English but does not literally follow any AI algorithms, to convince us that following algorithms is *not always even part* of the explanation of understanding English. To show that something is not always part of an explanation of something, one needs to show that it is not a *necessary* condition! In the present case then, it is the fact that some of us speak Chinese, but do not at the same time literally and consciously push addresses on stacks that shows that we do not speak Chinese *by* literally and consciously following AI algorithms.

For another example, suppose that I wanted to prove that I do not keep my balance on my bicycle *by* calculating solutions to partial differential equations. I would show this by riding my bicycle, while at the same time paying careful attention to whether or not I was also calculating solutions to partial differential equations. (To build a computer that would actually balance a bicycle, one would need to write a program that did include routines to do such calculations. But recall sec. 2 above; computers do not compute.) The fact that I balance the bicycle without doing the calculations shows that doing such calculations is not always a *necessary* condition for balancing the bicycle; and this shows that I do not always balance bicycles even in part *by* doing any such calculations.

This argument is similar to one given by Berkeley (sec. 12) against the view that we judge distance in part by using optical angles and trigonometry. But the question raised here is precisely one involving introspection and the possibility of following rules literally yet unconsciously. Berkeley just says that he above anyone else is the best judge of whether or not he is doing trigonometry problems, and he says that he isn't doing any such thing.

But is this sufficient to prove the point? Why can't we say that Berkeley was (literally but unconsciously) doing such computations?[4] Is there some way of literally, but not consciously, following these algorithms? Is there something in between literally and consciously obeying a rule and merely behaving in accordance with it? Does it

---

4 Those who think this makes no sense should consider the following game: players alternate selecting a card from an exposed pack containing nine cards, numbered 1-9. The first player to be able to make a total of exactly fifteen, using exactly three of the cards he has taken, is the winner. I claim that everyone has played this game hundreds of times, but without being aware of it (see Sharvy 1985).

make sense to say that some *part* of me literally *and consciously* follows algorithms, but that *I* am unconscious of this part?

Now Searle, when conversing in English, does not do so by consciously and literally following or obeying any instructions. But he is exhibiting regularities which can be represented by a large number of distinct algorithms. Thus, he is no different with respect to English than a computer that appears to converse in English. Both instantiate (weak sense) many programs; neither literally follows (strong sense) any program. The possibility of artificial intentionality remains an open question; but Searle was never attacking this in the first place. The point then is that whether or not metallic machines are ever built which possess intentionality, they will not do so *by* literally following programs either. But why should they? 4.2 billion *organic* 'machines' don't.

Instantiating a program *P* in the weak sense merely involves exhibiting a certain regularity expressed in *P*. Program *P may* fail to express a theory that explains what it is to be in state *C*; that is, *P may* fail to be a representation that explains *C*. But this fact is merely an instance of the more general truth of philosophy of science, that not every statement of a regularity constitutes an explanation.

Searle wanted to show that programs which cause computers to simulate a knowledge of English do not *explain* what it is to know English. He wanted to dispute the claim that AI programs 'explain human cognition' (417, col. 1) and 'human understanding' (418, col. 1). But this is a large step on Searle's part, which I believe is not justified. There might well be AI programs that explain and accurately represent what is involved in understanding English, even though a man could be locked in a room following the program without understanding English. Some regularity statements explain, and some do not. What Searle needed was a specific argument that AI programs merely describe regularities, but do not *explain* e.g., what it is to understand Chinese.

Of *course* the explanation of how I understand English is not that I do it *by* literally and consciously following an algorithm. But it is consistent with this that an explanation of how I understand English might be expressed and represented by an algorithm. Perhaps one of the many algorithms that expresses the regularities I exhibit in conversing in English also constitutes a good *theory* of what it is to understand English. The actual elements of the program could explain and reveal the structure of the soul's understanding of English. For example, the program might represent tree structures, recursive syntactic rules, etc. And the situation here is not peculiar to mental activity or intentionality. Billiard balls do not behave as they do *by* literally following the laws of physics. And they certainly do not behave as they do *by* exhibiting the regularities described in those laws, i.e., by behaving as they do. In fact, billiard balls do not behave as they do *by* doing anything. But those laws may still provide explanations of the motions of billiard balls.

The situation we are left with is familiar in the history of science. Something rule-like fits the observed data and accurately predicts future data. It is a useful representation of part of the world. But is it an *explanation*? Against strong AI claims, we simply note that successful simulations do not warrant claims that the representations therein provide such explanations. A theory can work, but still be a bad one. A theory can make accurate predictions, yet explain nothing.

And against Searle: suppose that we had a machine that was constructed on principles isomorphic with that of the human brain, but which could have patterns imprinted upon it via programs via compilers.[5] Would not Searle have to admit that such an item might literally understand English, despite the fact that a program was used in its construction? Yes (see Lycan's commentary, 435). And now the functionalist worry: consider a machine that was *not* constructed exactly like a human brain – consider a Martian's brain – don't we want to admit that these might have the same intentionalities that we

5 The relevant 'causal powers of the human brain' that Searle mentions should not involve its being made of carbon, nitrogen, etc. They should be the powers that come from the structure of the individual neurons, and their connections (422, col. 2). Of course a computer could simulate a neuron, or even a network of ten billion of them, but that would still be just a simulation of a brain. It might not be a real brain, and it might not have all the relevant causal powers of a real brain.

Unfortunately, there is now empirical evidence that the brain may have very little to do with thinking after all. John Lorber, a neurologist at Sheffield University, has found a number of normal, intelligent people who have virtually no brains at all (see Paterson).

do? Yes? How about a PDP-10? And if a PDP-10 came to literally understand English, wouldn't we look to the program for some understanding of how it did that? Yes. Of course that program might not provide an explanation of *human* understanding of English. And then again, it might.

Received December, 1982

BIBLIOGRAPHY

Berkeley, George (1709), *Essay Towards a New Theory of Vision*

Hofstadter, Douglas R., 'Reductionism and Religion' (comment on Searle). *BBS* **3** (1980) 433-4

Lycan, William G., 'The Functionalist Reply (Ohio State)' (comment on Searle). *BBS* **3** (1980) 434-5.

Paterson, David., 'Is Your Brain Really Necessary?' *World Medicine* **15**, (1980) 21-4

Plato, *Republic* VI

Quine, W.V. *World and Object*, Chap. VII. (Cambridge MS.: MIT 1960)

Searle, John R. 'Minds, brains, and programs.' *The Behavioral and Brain Sciences* **3** (1980) 417-57 (includes commentaries and replies). Reprinted in Douglas R. Hofstadter and Dandiel C. Dennett, eds., *The Mind's I*, (New York: Basic Books, 1981) 353-73; and in John Haugeland, ed., *Mind Design*, (Cambridge, MS.: MIT Press, Bradford Books, 1981) 282-306.

Sharvy, Richard. 'It Ain't the Meat, It's the Motion.' *Inquiry* **26** (1983) 125-31.

Sharvy, Richard, 'A Philosophy Experiment.' *Teaching Philosophy* (1984) forthcoming

Smythe, William E., 'Simulation Games' (comment on Searle). *BBS* **3** (1980) 448-9

Synge, J.L., *Talking about Relativity*. (Amsterdam: North Holland 1970)

CANADIAN JOURNAL OF PHILOSOPHY
Supplementary Volume 11

Dennett, Functionalism, and Introspection

WILLIAM LYONS
Trinity College
Dublin 2
Ireland

I

Recent functionalist accounts of the mental, at least on the part of philosophers, have often been a result of dissatisfaction with the reductionist accounts championed by such physicalists as Place, Smart and Feigl. In particular this new account gained momentum from the growing belief that our map of the mental, at least in regard to the higher cognitive functions, does not seem to be a map of the brain and its processes. The more we find out about the working brain, the less we are able to cling to the belief that our talk about beliefs, evaluations, intentions, desires and motives gives us information about the structure or functioning of our brains. The relation between the mental and the physical, if to talk of such a relation is not to misconstrue the nature of things, must be much more subtle and indirect than a correlation or identity or reduction of the mental to the physical. William James's positivist hope of making psychology into a science by using our privileged knowledge of events in our stream of consciousness as the means to identify the functioning of the underlying structures in the brain has been fulfilled in some respects but not in most. Wilder Penfield and others[1] were successful in using introspective reports as a guide to discovering the function of some areas in the brain, but it has since become clear that at most what was discovered was only part, though in some cases arguably a crucial part, of the functioning of the brain on such occasions. Further, in general, the higher (evolutionally speaking) the mental act or operation, the greater the complexity and the more widespread the system in the brain which is to be associated with that act or operation. The more the act becomes clearly cognitive, the more vague becomes our understanding of the role of any relevant brain states or operations, because our picture of such cognitive activities, often gained allegedly from introspection, gives us little or no guidance to discovering the relevant brain states or systems and their operations.

At any rate the result in both empirical and philosophical psychology was a move away from reductionism to a functionalist account of the mental. It is neither easy nor particularly important to try and locate an exact beginning of what has since been called the functionalist account of the mental.[2] Hilary Putnam's papers have certain-

1 See, for example, W. Penfield and T. Rasmussen *The Cerebral Cortex of Man: A Clinical Study of Localization of Function* (London: Macmillan 1957) and W. Penfield *The Excitable Cortex in Conscious Man*, The Sherrington Lectures No. 5 (Liverpool: Liverpool University Press 1958).

2 What might be seen as prototypes of recent functionalism in philosophy can be discerned in some of the Pragmatists. For example, in *Mind, Self and Society: From the Standpoint of a Social Behaviourist* (edit. C.V. Morris, Cambridge: Cambridge University Press 1934) G.H. Mead writes, 'I know of no way in which intelligence or mind could arise or could have arisen, other than through the internalization by the individual of social processes of experience and behaviour, that is, through this internalization of the conversation of significant gestures... And if mind or thought has arisen in this way, then there neither can be nor could have been any mind or thought without language; and

ly been of seminal importance in generating contemporary discussion about functionalist accounts of the mind.[3] For Putnam the relation of the mental to the physical is analogous to that of the functional description – or 'machine table'[4] – of a simple computer or Turing machine to the physical description of any particular realisation of it.[5] That is, one can describe a computer in terms of the various operations it can perform, and the ordering of operations for complex performances or computations, without mentioning (and while being indifferent to) whether the computer is made of plastic or wood, or even of people in an office organised into a smooth working unit. The 'machine table' can be fully described in terms of the relations between the various current states, plus inputs and outputs, and these relations in turn can be described entirely in logico-linguistic terms. Thus the computer has properties only describable in terms of its 'machine table,' and properties only describable in terms of its physical structure. Similarly humans have 'abstract properties'[6] only describable in

---

the early stages of the development of language must have been prior to the development of mind or thought' (191-2). On the other hand, contemporary functionalists do not make reference to nor give acknowledgement to Mead or any of the other Pragmatists of that period. Quite likely, modern functionalism has been generated more or less entirely in response to contemporary concerns.

3 The classical papers by Putnam on functionalism are 'Minds and machines' (1961), 'Robots: machines or artificially created life?' (1964), 'Brains and behaviour' (1965), 'The mental life of some machines' (1967), 'The nature of mental states' (1967), and 'Philosophy and our mental life' (1973), all of which appear in Putnam *Mind, Language and Reality*, Philosophical Papers, Vol. 2 (Cambridge: Cambridge University Press 1976).

4 The tabulation of the machine's outputs in terms of columns representing internal states and rows representing input instructions. The intersection of the input instruction and current state gives the output displayed in the square at the point of intersection.

5 Putnam explains this analogy in most detail in 'Minds and machines,' originally published in *Dimensions of Mind: A Symposium*, S. Hook, ed. (New York: Collier Books 1961).

6 Putnam's account as to why these properties are 'real and autonomous features of our world' is perhaps best displayed in 'Philosophy and our mental life' in *Mind, Language and Reality* above.

terms of their psychological functioning, and concrete properties only describable in terms of their physiology. Two computers, or two humans, can be functionally isomorphic[7] but quite different in physical constitution. Indeed in the future a computer or robot might be made functionally isomorphic with a human, but this functioning might be realised in the robot in a physical way quite different from human physiology. The mental life of humans is their 'machine table,' so to speak.

We do not as yet know a human's 'machine table' because we do not yet have a good, much less a complete, psychological theory of humans. We do not yet have a comprehensive 'programme' for the brain. Part of the reason for this is that to talk thus about a human's 'machine table' is to talk in terms of an inexact analogue for human psychology. Humans are not a simple closed programmed system such that one can speak literally of a 'machine table' or 'programme' for them. Humans are a 'hotch potch' of many overlapping or discrete, interlocking or clashing or simply unconnected systems. If a human is at one and the same time angry, intending to have dinner, hoping for rain, and a pessimist, it is unlikely that one could ever refer to a single programme as explanation for what the human is likely to do at that time.[8] Moreover, whatever might turn out to be the best functional model of humans' higher cognitive activities, such a model may be indifferent to any particular realisation in terms of brain function because it is so formalised and idealised that it bears little or no relation to what actually goes on in the brain. A functional psychological model is something that enables us to plot and make sense of human activity. Its restrictions and limits are determined by whether it makes good sense and is a good explanation, not by the neurohpysiology of the brain. In that sense, as Putnam puts it, 'we have what we always

---

7 In 'Philosophy and our mental life', page 294, Putnam explains the notion of functional isomorphism by saying 'that two systems are functionally isomorphic if there is an isomorphism that makes both of them models for the same psychological theory ... they are isomorphic realizations of the same abstract structure.'

8 Putnam deals with the drawbacks to the computer-human analogy in 'Philosophy and our mental life', 298 ff.

wanted – an autonomous mental life. And we need no mysteries, no ghostly agents, no *elan vital* to have it.'[9] And that is more or less where Putnam's speculations end. He does not proffer many details about how particular mental acts or processes are to be explained under this model. In particular he gives us no more than a few passing hints as to how introspection might be treated and never directly addresses himself to that problem.[10]

II

Daniel Dennett, on the other hand, in one of the other classical sources for a functionalist view of mind, *Content and Consciousness*, directs special attention to consciousness and introspection precisely because they are connected with 'the feature of the mind that is most resistant to absorption into the mechanistic picture of science,'[11] namely intentionality, the fact that mental activities possess some end or other activity as their content, and he too looks to computers as the most useful analogue for what he wants to explain.

Dennett explains that to try to correlate mental talk with brain events is to mistake the nature and origin of mental talk. To illustrate his view, consider the case when one describes a zebra as having realised it was in danger. The use of the word 'realised' – a mental, intentional term – is on the basis of our knowledge of the context or environmental conditions at the time plus our kowledge of how the animal reacted to them. We say that the zebra realised that it was in danger because there was in its line of vision, and upwind from it, a large lioness, and because the zebra raised its head, sniffed the air,

9 'Philosophy and our mental life', 303

10 In 'Minds and machines' in *Dimensions of Mind*, 146 ff.

11 *Content and Consciousness* (London: Routledge and Kegan Paul 1969), 40. Another more recent functionalist account of introspection is to be found in Stephen N. Thomas, *The Formal Mechanics of Mind*, Harvester Studies in Cognitive Science (Brighton: Harvester Press 1978) Part I, section 5.

made certain noises and then took to its heels in the opposite direction. The response was appropriate to the dangerous situation; it was cognitively correct, so we can use the appropriate mental phrase 'realised it was in danger' of the zebra.

> *What the animal was doing* ... can only be told in Intentional terms, but it is not a story about features of the world *in addition to* the features of the extensional story; it just describes what happens in a different way.[12]

So it should be clear that to consider mental talk as oblique or even inexact and prescientific reference to brain activity is to be ignorant of how and why we attribute mental acts. Mental or intentional attribution is made on the basis of the large view of what some behaving organism is up to, which in turn can only be made sense of by considering the context, the organism, and the resulting behaviour. Further, this behaviour must be understood in the light of its usual successful outcome (again in the long term and in general) if one is to give some substance to the words 'appropriate' and 'correct' in the phrases 'appropriate behaviour' and 'cognitively correct.' Mental talk is not poor quality talk about brains, or even poor quality guessing about what goes on inside some animal's brain, it is talk about the animal in the large context of usual appropriate responses to noted stimuli. In our mental talk we may occasionally say that realising, as well as believing and hoping and guessing, 'go on inside our head' or even that they are the content of our brain states, but such ascriptions are 'essentially a heuristic overlay on the extensional theory rather than intervening variables of the theory.'[13] Mental talk is making sense of what goes on in our head in the light of input and output. To imagine that our mental talk can lead us to make predictions about what animals or people will do, which could not be made on the basis of the empirical (or extensional as opposed to intentional), knowledge we have of those animals or people is to put the cart before the horse. Just as the cart must (almost) always follow the horse (at least causally

---

12 *Content and Consciousness,* 78

13 *Content and Consciousness,* 80

speaking!) so must intentional explanations or mental talk be parasitic on our knowledge of the environment and an organism's appropriate response to it.

Before I proceed to examine Dennett's accounts of introspection, it should be pointed out that in the Introduction to *Brainstorms*,[14] he is at pains to distinguish his brand of functionalism from what he calls earlier 'Turing machine functionalism.' According to this earlier form of functionalism mental predicates are to be identified with functional predicates. If two people share the same belief then their shared mental state will be characterisable by the same functional description, which in turn can be couched in terms of a shared programme. Thus to be in the same mental state is to be at the same point in the working through of a shared programme.

Dennett suggests that Turing machine functionalism is implausible precisely because it interprets functionalism too narrowly and literally in terms of a programme. It is implausible because it is based on the assumption that, though we do not yet know its details and may never do so, nevertheless we all share the same programme in terms of which we organise information and behaviour. This assumption ignores the vast differences in the nature and nurture of individual humans. Think of the difference in upbringing of a native of the Fly River area in Papua New Guinea and of an inhabitant of Manhattan in New York. How could it be envisaged that these two share the same programme?

I am inclined to think that Dennett is exaggerating the difference between his own form of functionalism and Turing machine functionalism, and, in so doing, distorting the views of those, like Putnam, who first made the analogy between the mental and the computer's 'machine table.' Putnam at least, as we have seen, was at pains to point out that there probably is not and, strictly speaking could not be, a single programme for humans, and that the original analogy must not be carried too far.

---

14 *Brainstorms: Philosophical Essays on Mind and Psychology* (Brighton: Harvester Press 1979); there are also arguments against Turing machine functionalism in N.J. Block and J.R. Fodor 'What psychological states are not,' *Philosophical Review*, **81** (1972) esp. Part III.

However it might be suggested that there is a much more important worry about the mind-programme analogy, namely that a computer does not function intentionally. It merely processes information and carries out instructions without understanding or believing or planning or being in any intentional states; it manipulates formal symbols without understanding the interpretation of the symbols. The *programmer* understands the interpretation, as does the person who interprets the output, but the computer does not. Thus, it might be argued, it is misleading to view the mental as merely the brain's computational programme.

John Searle, in his article 'Minds, Brains and Programs,'[15] has produced a powerful argument to underline this worry. Searle proposed the following thought experiment (I will give it in slightly adapted form): An English-speaking person who does not understand Chinese is placed in a room in which there is stored a complete set of Chinese characters plus a set of instructions in English as regards which written characters to push out under the door whenever a particular combination of characters is fed in under the door. Clearly an observer, outside the room, who did not know who or what was inside the room, would most likely be fooled into thinking that the room contained someone who understood Chinese (or else that 'the room' did!). Equally clearly the person in the room does not understand a single character but merely follows faithfully the instructions about how to manipulate output in the light of input.

But does Searle's argument really cast doubt on the mind-programme analogy and so on functional interpretations of the mental? While our intuitions baulk at suggesting that the person in the room understands Chinese, should we refuse to admit that the complex of prepared instructions, person in the room, and store of characters, lacks understanding? Our intuitions – used to attributing understanding to persons – might indeed baulk, but should they *stop* us attributing understanding to such a system? It might be suggested

---

15 In *The Behavioral and Brain Sciences*, **3** (1980); Hofstadter and Dennett take it seriously enough to reprint it and attempt a rebuttal in D. Hofstadter and D. Dennett *The Mind's I: Fantasies and Reflections on Self and Soul* (Brighton: Harvester Press 1981).

that they should not, because after all the instructions had to be written by someone who does understand Chinese (otherwise the whole thing would have to be put down to magic), and so the instructions are generated by and incorporate understanding. Thus the complex – the set of instructions, plus the person in the room carrying them out, plus the store of Chinese characters – does have or 'embody' or 'contain' understanding of Chinese.

Now Searle could grant that while the *complex* has understanding, it should also be clear that, by himself, the person in the room who carries out the instructions – who engages merely in 'formal symbol manipulation' – does not have understanding. Further, and this is his main point, to characterise a person's mental operations in a purely functional way is like characterising that person's mind as if it were an inner room in which a computer merely carried out instructions, that is, followed a programme. (Waggishly, Searle has remarked that if mere processing of output in the light of input is the criterion, then our stomachs are cognitive systems.)

Now this argument of Searle's, it seems to me, does count against Turing machine or computer functionalism but not against unreduced 'intentional system' functionalism, for this latter version describes our cognitive functions in terms of intentional items, that is, states like believing, knowing, understanding, etc. which already incorporate understanding as part of their characterisation. But to remain at the level of unreduced 'intentional systems' would be to do so at great cost. It would entail giving up the goal – which Dennett shares – of absorbing the mental wholly into 'the mechanistic picture of science,' for to remain at the level of unreduced 'intentional systems' is to fail to produce a purely functional account. To say so-and-so has a belief is not merely to connect input to output by way of a followed instruction to do something. A belief, besides involving (always?) a 'motor set' – or readiness to behave in a certain way in suitable circumstances – involves understanding a content (usually expressible in propositional form), and this in turn is usually characterised as some form of endorsement (itself an intentional concept) of that content as true or as being the best available hypothesis.

The whole-hearted acceptance of the considerations underlined by Searle's thought experiment would lead to a permanent dilution of hardline computer functionalism in the direction of intentional system functionalism. The acceptance of Searle's argument in effect would present a functionalist with a dilemma: To stick at the intentional system level is to fail to mesh the mental with the mechanistic physical sciences and to run the risk of giving comfort to Cartesian psychologies; to move from the intentional system stance back into the reductionist stance of pure computer functionalism is to be confronted with Searle-like arguments and, in general, to leave oneself open to the charge of having given an unconvincing portrayal of the mental. Dennett, as we shall see, was clearly alert to these tensions and could be interpreted as attempting to keep a foot planted in both positions, believing that he could do so without permanent philosophical injury because he was not attempting to keep his feet in both positions *at the same time*. He believed that, initially, to preserve intentionality in our functional characterisation of the mental, one must take up the 'intentional system' stance or the 'intentional stance' and describe mental functions in terms of such ordinary 'folk psychological' intentional terms as beliefs, hopes, and desires. Eventually, as our understanding of these operations became deeper, we could replace the intentional characterisation of each one with an account of (probably of a series of) non-intentional subroutines or processes. It would be a little like gradually replacing the neuronal circuits of our brains by microchips but at the same time preserving what, at the top or macro level, we describe as our ability to believe, hope, desire, understand, etc. In so far as this possibility of replacing the intentional with a complex of non-intentional subroutines remains plausible, the functionalist has an answer to Searle. The 'Chinese Room' will eventually embody intentionality when the instructions to carry out the routines involving Chinese characters become complex enough to mirror the myriad subroutines which a functionalist believes can incorporate the essence of understanding Chinese. But I shall discuss this crucial aspect of functionalism again when I come to consider Dennett's model of introspection in detail.

At any rate Dennett maintains that the original Turing machine or computer analogy was and still is illuminating, important and *basically* right. The best way, the correct way of characterising the mental is in functional terms. It is just that it must be remembered that this account of the mental is much more open and messy than Turing machine functionalism seems to suggest. Mental states cannot be identified or picked out against a background of a clear and agreed and shared programme for humans because there is no such shared computational programme. At most what we can say is that we all have (what at present must be characterised as) a roughly similar intentional system but not the exact same one. An intentional system is a first-stage functional characterisation of the mental and is made up of intentional items (such as beliefs, wishes, hopes, desires), some of which will be lifted more or less untouched from 'folk psychology' and bear our current mental terms, some of which will not. Further some of our current mental terms will not feature in any description of the system at all but must be eliminated as too ghostly and Cartesian for honourable mention at any stage. The (at least initially) acceptable items – let us for the moment allow that belief and desire are such items[16] – are to be grouped together as a system because it is possible in terms of the functioning of these items and the (rationally conceived) interrelations between them, to predict the behaviour of something to which such items are correctly attributed. We cannot attribute, then, a specific programme to all organisms or things of a certain kind – to all humans, for example – we can only attribute to a specific human whatever beliefs and desires, for instance, it seems sensible to attribute to him given that he is human, given our knowledge of his history (his culture, education, etc.), and given reasonably accurate knowledge of the sort of information he must be taken to possess and the spectrum of goals he can be supposed to have. We can only predict what he will do if he can then be supposed to act rationally in respect of his beliefs, desires and goals. We take up the intentional stance in regard to a person and attribute to him or her an intentional system. There is no grand intentional system or programme which a person must be said to have, and so no grand view of the spectrum of mental events. Thus, Dennett asserts, 'the details of my view [of the mental] must for this reason be built up piecemeal, by case studies and individual defences that are not intended to generalise to all mental entities and all mental states.'[17]

---

16 In *Brainstorms*, xx, Dennett suggests that such items would not appear in 'a mature psychology.'

17 *Ibid*. The elaboration of the notion of an intentional system is in *Brainstorms*, Part I, ch. 1.

III

So it is time to look at Dennett's case study of introspection. His first elaborated account occurs in *Content and Consciousness*,[18] and this account becomes the foundation for his subsequent construction of a functionalist model of consciousness. For Dennett, according to this first account, the essential feature of introspection is that it delivers error-free reports of functionally characterised inner states. Indeed the key to understanding introspection lies in the correct account of how and why such reports are infallible.

Dennett suggests that the human person is like a perceiving machine which registers whatever impinges on its perceptual apparatus or organs. Such a machine does not depict the outside world on some screen in an inner cinema – for who would view it? – but, via an analyser, produces intentionally analysed and edited verbally-expressible accounts of the outside world. The machine can be tricked into generating false descriptions, say by placing a cardboard cutout soldier next to a real one amid some undergrowth at a distance of a hundred yards from the perceiver. The perceptual apparatus, with its analyser, will most likely generate a description of two soldiers deployed in undergrowth. But once that descriptive account is generated without malfunction by the analyser, and given that no extraneous content is fed into the speech centre along with the contents of the analyser – no hunches, guesses, prejudices, or presuppositions – then the only other possible error that can occur, when the machine gives an 'introspective' account of what it has seen, is verbal error. Strictly speaking, *only* the latter sort of error directly pertains to introspection. For to introspect is not to *report* on the contents of the analyser, with the attendant possibility of misreporting, but it is, after the analyser is hooked up to the speech centre and its contents fed into the speech centre, merely to *printout* those contents. There is no further processing, after the contents of the analyser (or any other contents) are fed into the speech centre. All that occurs in introspection is that the speech centre's contents are printed out in 'introspective

18 The following account is culled from *Content and Consciousness*, chs. V-VIII.

reports.' This printing-out facility can malfunction – make a verbal slip, so to speak – but it cannot mis-see, mis-inspect, mis-retro-spect, mis-report, or mis-identify, because there are no such mysterious ghostly processes going on. Thus, barring verbal slips, introspection must be error free.

This account of introspection is the basis of Dennett's account of consciousness or awareness. There are, he alleges, two levels and so two concepts of awareness, and the blurring of these in ordinary speech generates the paradoxes in our ordinary conception of consciousness. One is $aware_2$ (or conscious at the lower level) of something if one has input from that thing (object or event) into the 'perceptual analyser,' and so can organise and control one's behaviour in terms of it, but the ensuing analysed content may not be passed on into the 'speech centre.' One is $aware_1$ (or conscious at the higher level) of that thing if and when input from it is passed on into the 'speech centre' and so becomes accessible to introspection, i.e., can be 'printed out' in our introspective talk. Insects and birds, and most animals, are $aware_2$ but not $aware_1$ because they do not have a speech centre and so cannot introspect.[19] Humans on the other hand have both levels of consciousness. However even with humans it should be emphasised that the introspective printout of internal computations, such as reasoning in general or mental arithmetic in particular, is an intentionally analysed and edited version of what the brain does which has been fed into the speech centre. We can say that we first multiplied seven by four, then added two, and so on, but we do not know how we multiplied seven by four. Did we print out serially four lots of seven units and then add them up, or did we refer to a line in an embedded version of the seven times tables, or what?

---

19 Dennett also discusses $consciousness_1$ and $consciousness_2$ in his 'Reply to Arbib and Gunderson' in *Brainstorms*, and remarks there, in a footnote, that he still maintains the distinction.

IV

In *Brainstorms,* first published nearly ten years after *Content and Consciousness,* Dennett has given up the very ground on which he had built his first functionalist account of introspection - namely that it delivers error-free reports of functionally characterised inner states – and so elaborated a significantly different functionalist model of introspection. In the light of the history of psychology, it is very difficult, indeed highly implausible, to maintain that introspection delivers error-free reports, and so I believe that Dennett was right to rebuild his model of introspection so as to accomodate its unreliability. As he put it in *Brainstorms,*[20] there is a world of difference between 'our feelings of special authority in offering introspection reports' – which stem from the fact that we have the ability to report accurately on what is available to us (in the speech centre) to report – and the ability to report accurately on our internal data, computations and decisions.

In *Content and Consciousness* Dennett had limited the introspective process to the process of printing out what was in the speech centre, or 'out tray.' In a sense he was driven to do this by having first committed himself to the proposition that introspection was free from error. As he realised that all sorts of editing, censoring, glossing and interpreting could go on before the material got to the 'out tray' – that the resulting manuscript was more likely to be palimpsest than original codex – this meant (unless he were to give up the error-free thesis) that introspection must refer only to the more or less uninterruptible and automatic process of posting what was in the 'out tray' (or publishing what was in the speech centre). Freedom from error was gained at considerable cost. Strictly speaking, introspection was no longer *reporting* of any sort, but just a process of *publishing*. There was no searching or discovering or collecting or inspecting or retrospecting or anything of that sort in the process to which the label 'introspection' properly applied. To preserve the freedom from error of introspection, Dennett realised, one had to emasculate the process.

---

20 The retraction occurs in *Brainstorms,* 171.

So, by giving up the error-free criterion in *Brainstorms*, the way was now open for a more potent and convincing account of introspection.[21] As one has come to expect in regard to functionalist theories, the new model of introspection is expounded in the language of computer software:

> Suppose Control [a higher executive component in the brain] 'decides' for various reasons to 'introspect':
>
> (1) it goes into its introspection subroutine, in which
>
> (2) it directs a question to M [short-term or buffer memory];
>
> (3) when an answer comes back (and none may) it assesses, the answer: it may
>
> (a) censor the answer
>
> (b) 'interpret' the answer in the light of other information
>
> (c) 'draw inferences' from the answer, or
>
> (d) relay the answer as retrieved direct to PR [a 'public relations' or printout component].
>
> (4) The outcome of any of (a-d) can be a speech command to PR.
>
> The point of the buffer memory M is that getting some item of information in M is a necessary but not a sufficient condition for getting it accessed by PR in the form of the *content* of some speech act command.[22]

This theory clearly makes room for and allows for some explanation of the unreliability of introspection. Introspective reports can fail to mention internal information received or processes performed, or they

21 The account is taken from *Brainstorms*, Part II, ch. 9, 'Towards a cognitive theory of consciousness,' and should be read in conjunction with Dennett's article 'On the absence of phenomenology,' in *Body, Mind, and Method*, D.F. Gustafson and B.L. Tapscott eds. (Dordrecht: D. Reidel 1979).

22 *Brainstorms*, 156

can give edited 'bitty' versions of them, or they can give interpreted, biased, 'loaded' versions of them. Introspective reports can mention information or processes which have not taken place, for Control can mistake a hunch or hope or expectation of an event for its occurrence, and place such material in PR in such a way that it is then indistinguishable from factual material and so is issued as fact. On this model, introspection is the series of processes whereby Control, the higher executive component in the brain, directs questions to memory, sifts and edits the answers if necessary, and passes on the material to the speech centre which, if so commanded, in turn publishes it. Introspection is now genuinely a process of *reporting* on what has been stored in memory as regards events perceived, and internal computations, plans, and decisions made, albeit with the proviso that between these internal states and Control, and between Control and lip, there may be many a slip.

Another important aspect of Dennett's model is that it entails that we do not have direct and immediate introspective access to mental processes as they happen but only to some version of them stored in memory. That is why the processes of introspection are best represented, he seems to be suggesting, not as a direct scanning or monitoring of first-order processes, but as asking questions and receiving answers. Introspection may deliver a series of consecutive answers related to the same process or series of processes, and this may look like direct and immediate access to the process itself, just as a series of light flashes in linear sequence can look like a single travelling light source. So, of course, because of introspective evidence, we may *think* that we are directly registering internal mental processes, and so all too easily fall prey to talking about 'perceiving' with the 'inner eye.'

In fact it does not follow from Dennett's claim that we do not have direct and immediate access to first order mental processes, that the result must be that our information about such processes can amount to no more than discrete 'snapshots' of what is really a process already completed. For memory might plausibly be construed – at least in regard to introspection – as more like an 'instant replay' facility whose answers to questions comprise (continuous) replays of the original processes.

Dennett went on to suggest that 'that of which we are conscious is that of which we can tell, introspectively or retrospectively,'[23] that is, he tied awareness or consciousness$_1$ – consciousness at the higher level – to introspection once again. Thus creatures who cannot tell (i.e., have no language), are not conscious in the full or higher sense of the term precisely because they cannot introspectively report.

This may seem to be an unnecessary hostage to fortune. Since, on this account, the more important processes of introspection are Control's getting and sifting answers from Memory, why did Dennett not define ordinary consciousness as the ability to get such answers, so that one could be conscious in the full sense of something inner but not be able to tell? The answer, I suspect, is that we do not ordinarily claim to be aware of such complex processing – of actually retrieving material from storage, of asking questions or, in general, of engaging in the subroutines we engage in – but we do claim awareness of what we are about to tell, of what is in the speech centre (though not *as* being in the speech centre), that is, of what is 'on the tip of one's tongue,' waiting to be included in an introspective report. For the purposes of consciousness or awareness, the emphasis must be placed on what is in the speech centre, ready to be told more or less immediately. Dennett's position is the reverse of William James, who held that introspection was parasitic on consciousness because the proper account of introspection was in terms of a stream of contents of consciousness of which we are aware. Introspection was access to that stream of consciousness, albeit at one remove when it was frozen in memory. Dennett's position is that consciousness is parasitic on introspection, which in turn is explained as a routine by means of which a person gains access to and reports on the contents of his or her buffer memory, albeit at times in censored or biased or tampered form.

V

While the functionalist approach to the mental is undeniably attractive, it is time now to look carefully at the model of introspection that

---

23 *Brainstorms*, 152

has resulted from this approach. Inevitably this examination will also yield comments about the functionalist approach in general, and I shall begin with a problem that does just that, for I shall point up some of the conflicts that appear in Dennett's account of introspection in the light of his overall strategy of explanation of the mental in terms of intentional systems.

If to characterise mental states and processes functionally, according to Dennett, is to locate them as part of an intentional system, which in turn is to give an explanation in terms of a complex constructed out of beliefs, hopes, desires and the other rough and ready items of our ordinary quotidian 'folk psychology,' how is his explanation of introspection (in terms of Control sending questions to memory and sifting and analysing and censoring and editing) a genuine Dennettian functionalist account? It might be objected that such an account is supposed to be a stiffened-up part of 'folk psychology,' that is, a systematised version of some more or less common intentional explanation that has been used over the centuries as a means to understanding the behaviour of ourselves and others. But there is nothing at all in the 'folk psychological' account of introspection about (or even equivalent to) Control, buffer memeory, editing, censoring, interpreting, printing-out, and so on.

The answer lies in the fact that, as we have seen, Dennett also envisages an eventual reduction of higher-level intentional systems to lower-level, non-intentional, mechanistic, science-compatible systems. So, as merely a downward stage on this programme, presumably, Dennett has reverted in part to the analogy between computers and humans, that is, he has thus conceived of introspection for the time being in terms of a model such as those working in artificial intelligence might produce. Though he makes no specific claims about how Control, Memory, speech centre, print-out, and so on are incarnated in the brain, it would follow from his general programme that – and here he departs from the aims of many of those working in artificial intelligence – he is putting this account forward (at least when the reductive programme is complete) as a correct functional account of human introspection. That is, ultimately, he will be putting forward what he believes is a correct description of the moves which our brain makes; though *how* it makes them – how in detail the brain works – is another matter, a matter for neurophysiology.

To put this another way, Dennett seems to want to inject an eliminative materialist strand into his intentional systematising because he intends his account to be assimilable to and so his work to be relevant to the brain sciences. Ultimately he wants his models to be 'sub-personal,' that is, to explain personal behaviour 'by analysing a person into an organisation of subsystems (organs, routines, nerves, faculties, components – even atoms),' which are not the subjects of ordinary personal experience,[24] but he also wants them to portray accurately how the brain works. Thus, in explaining the details of his model of introspection, Dennett refers to 'feature detectors' and points out that brain scientists claim to have discovered these to be part of the structures by means of which we perceive the external world; and when explaining the function of Control, he draws on evidence from experimental psychology for the existence of an executive component in the brain which controls the flow of information in the brain and directs its analysis.[25]

However, and this is the point of broaching these more general considerations, this programme of ultimately reducing intentional systems to non-intentional ones can be seen as a necessary move to allay a worry in regard to explanations in terms of intentional systems proper, namely whether there are sufficient limitations on what can count as an acceptable explanation for any such explanation to be said genuinely to explain. But, as we shall see in due course, in soothing away this worry he creates another one.

The worry in regard to intentional systems proper (or pure intentional systems explanations) arises in the following way. We should recall that, for Dennett, an intentional system explanation is not so much an inference to the correct explanation (in the sense of *the* explanation of how the human mind works) as an inference to the most coherent explanation in functional intentional terms of why that

24 *Brainstorms,* 153

25 Dennett refers to the experimental work of J.R. Lackner and M. Garrett 'Resolving ambiguity: Effects of biasing context in the unattended ear', *Cognition,* 1 (1973) and D. Broadbent *Perception and Communication* (London: Pergamon Press 1958).

behavioural output followed that environmental input. The resulting explanation will be in terms of 'putative events, states, achievements, processes,' which are 'idealised fictions in an action-predicting, action-explaining calculus.'[26] But in giving such explanations he now has the problem of finding a good reason why anyone should accept *his* 'idealised fiction' in regard to what goes on when we introspect rather than your one, or the version the grocer at the corner might produce when in reflective mood. Explanations in terms of intentional systems proper, according to Dennett, are anomalous *and* autonomous. Such explanations not only repudiate psychophysical correlations of a lawlike sort, but seem to demand that there be no constraints at all to be acknowledged from the direction of the brain. A purely intentional system is a free-floating explanation which is indifferent to possible physical realisations. It is an 'idealised fiction' upon which is placed only the constraints that it be rational and coherent, and explain output in terms of input. Dennett realised that it would follow from this that we could reasonably ask why we should endorse his account of introspection (and 'endorse' seems the best word here rather than, say, 'deem correct,' which might suggest that there was a sense in which one could check an intentional system explanation for accuracy).

Why indeed should we endorse Dennett's account of introspection in terms of Control, buffer memory, putting questions, receiving answers, censoring, interpreting, drawing inferences from, and publishing, rather than one like Armstrong's[27] in terms of some scanning device, with scrambler or encoder added, perhaps an interpreter as well, and then reporter? A suggestion that his explanation in terms of Control, buffer memory, and so on, is a priori more rational and coherent than other rival explanations that are equally comprehensive and explanatory of output in the light of input is not easy to maintain. A priori there must be little to choose in terms of 'rationality and

---

26 In Dennett's 'Reply to Arbib and Gunderson', *Brainstorms*, 30.

27 *A Materialist Theory of the Mind*, (London: Routledge and Kegan Paul 1968), ch. 6, sections X and XI, ch. 15. It should be noted that Armstrong's causal materialist account is here being considered as if it were merely a free-floating functionalist account.

coherence' between his explanation, Armstrong's, or a dozen other possibilities. For example, without loss of rationality or coherence, one could immediately substitute for Control a well organised Committee where one member does the questioning, another the editing, and so on. Or again, once could do away with Control or Committee and postulate that the various processes previously under the thumb of Control or Committee now proceed automatically according to 'wired in' procedures.

So in regard to introspection the limitations imposed by having to make one's explanation explanatory of behavioural output in the light of environmental input seem particularly minimal. Introspection is not a process that seems to be aimed directly at generating appropriate output. It is precisely because introspection is very often such a self-contained internal process that it causes such difficulties for functionalism. One can introspect quite independently of what is going on in the environment and without producing any 'motor set.' One can close one's eyes and think of England, and then introspect one's thinking. Or one might run over some scene witnessed last week, wondering why it has stuck in the memory. Of course introspection can be useful for planning behaviour, but it can also be disengaged from circumstance in a way that, say, most deliberating, decision-making, evaluation, and emotion are not. Introspection is often the mind in purely reflective mode. An introspective person is often an introverted person.

So the temptation for a functionalist to allay this worry by looking for further constraints on one's model is very strong in the case of introspection and the obvious first place to seek such constraints is from the direction of the brain. The temptation to be an eliminative materialist cum brain scientist must be all but overwhelming when one has succeeded in making the move from giving an explanation at the personal intentional level to one at the sub-personal level in terms of components, routines, and printouts. For when one de-intentionalises intentional system accounts, one cannot replace the intentional processes with just *any* series of non-intentional mechanistic processes which would produce the same output from the same input. For if one replaced the intentional processes merely with some rational and coherent series of subroutines, this series may only imitate or simulate a human intentional act functionally rather than reproduce it. It may only act as a good substitute for what the human intentional act does. But the brain may work in a quite different way; perhaps in a much more messy, less coherent, non-economic, non-rational way. To simulate the part played by human intentionality by means of non-intentional mechanistic processes would not show that this is what humans do when they engage in intentional activity. For this reason the temptation for a functionalist to be a brain scientist must be quite strong. For his account or model of something such as introspection only becomes useful and important – rather than just a clever simulation – in so far as it sheds light on how humans, human brains, *in fact* engage in intentional activities. The functionalist in philosophical psychology should try to produce not a simulation but a duplication which is explanatory and revealing of psychological reality.

However – and here is a new worry Dennett has generated in the process of stilling the old one – to yield to the temptation to be a brain scientist is to land back in the eliminative materialist camp whose problems functionalism was designed to avoid. If, in order to be aligned with explanations in the 'hard' sciences, intentional system accounts must be reduced ultimately to mechanistic accounts, *and* if such accounts will only be of real interest if they dupblicate how the brain works, then Dennettian functionalism collapses into eliminative materialism, for in effect it is committed to reducing our 'folk psychological' account of the mental, via an intentional system account, to an account in terms of brain states and processes. To the 'true blue' functionalist this is philosophical recidivism.

I want to look now at some of the finer details of Dennett's functionalist case study of introspection. In the first place I want to bring forward again a matter which I have already referred to as an unnecessary hostage to fortune on Dennett's part. I refer to his insistence that introspection does not and cannot take place unless one can get the information from perception or subsequent deliberation into the speech centre and publish it verbally, and that consciousness in the full sense (consciousness$_1$) is parasitic on this account of introspection. Intuitively this seems very odd, and close to a reductio ad absurdum of this model of introspection and consciousness, as Dennett seems to realise when he coyly admits that he will be taken to be the 'Village Verificationist.' For, given his view of consciousness in the full sense (consciousness$_1$), it entails that children, some deaf-mutes, and dogs, being without the ability to employ language, cannot publish verbally the contents of perception or internal computation and so cannot be conscious (conscious$_1$). This is odd because it seems fair to say that we take it as one of the facts which an adequate account of introspection and consciousness must cope with, that children and deaf-mutes are fully conscious and able to introspect.

In fact I believe that Dennett has no need at all to play the 'Village Verificationist' and why this is so may become clear from a consideration of a passage in *The Principles of Psychology*.[28] In this passage James refers to the now famous childhood experiences of a deaf and dumb man, Mr. Ballard, who later – when he had learnt sign language – related that, before he could convey thoughts and feelings to his parents and brothers other than 'by natural signs and pantomime,' he had a rich inner life woven out of his tactile and visual experiences. This inner life included metaphysical speculations about the origin of life and of the world itself which he was *un*able to communicate by means of natural signs and pantomime.[29] While Mr. Ballard does not mention specifically that he introspected his thoughts as well, nevertheless, since he clearly enjoyed reflective thinking of a most abstract kind, there is no obvious reason to believe that he was incapable of introspection or that he was not fully conscious.

However, at least with a comparatively small adjustment to his account, Dennett could accomodate the Ballard case, (and the case of children who have yet to learn a language.) As Mr. Ballard was able *later* to report on his pre-language metaphysical speculations and introspections, it could be argued that he must have stored the contents of these speculations and introspections in his speech centre or at least stored them in some language-compatible way. Thus, if Mr. Ballard was conscious and could introspect before he learnt sign language, Dennett could say that it was because he could put his thoughts into

28 *The Principles of Psychology* (New York: Dover 1950), vol. I, 266 ff.

29 On this point, see Samuel Porter 'Is thought possible without language? Case of a deaf-mute,' *The Princeton Review*, 57 (1881). This was James's source for the Ballard case. See also James 'Thought before language: A deaf-mute's recollections' *Philosophical Review*, I (1892).

linguistic form in an etiolated sense; that is, he could put them in storage in a form such that later they could be published via language of some sort.

In effect Dennett's view would now be that someone is occurrently $conscious_1$ if he (or she) can put the contents of his current thoughts into his speech centre (or into language-compatible storage) irrespective of whether now he has the ability to speak or, in general, to publish the contents of his speech centre. So unless Dennett stipulates that children and deaf-mutes who have yet to learn language do not yet have a speech centre, which would be very odd, he can easily accomodate the case of pre-language children and deaf-mutes. (The case of dogs is clearly more difficult, unless he allows them some form of language or at least publication of what they think and perceive. Could he not allow that canine behaviour of certain sorts is revelatory in a sufficiently controlled and directed manner of dog thoughts, or 'thoughts,' and perceptions?)

There is another more important puzzle in the details of Dennett's account of introspection as a sub-personal routine. In describing Control as assessing, directing questions, censoring, inferring, interpreting – albeit in inverted commas – he has underlined the confusion about the nature of his explanation, for he is clearly mixing the sub-personal with the personal. While Control – an 'executive component' in the brain, recall – and its activities are unknown to us in our personal life, he describes the activities of Control in everyday terms. It seems odd, having imported into his account the sub-personal mechanistic item Control, he then describes its functions in personal intentional terms. Control turns out to be an homunculus with intentional attitudes in disguise; not a higher executive component in the brain but a miniscule executive sitting at his desk in the brain. Now to claim to *explain* how introspectively we find out about the contents of our conscious thoughts, desires, and intentions, by claiming that we have within our heads a subpersonal component that asks questions and receives answers, assesses and interprets or censors them, and so on, is an odd claim indeed.[30]

---

30 In his paper 'Dennett on awareness,' *Philosophical Studies*, **23** (1972), Richard Rorty expresses related doubts concerning Dennett's use of the items 'analyser'

Dennett's response to this sort of complaint would be, most likely, that the intentionality still remaining at the first stage of analysis, or at any other intervening stages, will be eliminated once such items are reduced to the rock-bottom level of analytic explanation. The underlying claim is that an intentional item differs from a non-intentional one only in terms of complexity, so that when the complexity of an intentional item is fully displayed ipso facto it will be seen to have been reduced to a series of mechanistic non-intentional subroutines. Intentionality will turn out to be merely part of the surface-level or macro description which we now give to what in future we may be able to describe (and will be more accurately and scientifically described) as a complex organised subsystem or series of subroutines of a mechanistic sort. Intentionality is not an emergent property of the complex subsystem but merely a higher level way of describing it (which is ultimately misleading).

However, to be paradoxical, the complexity referred to above will be complex. It will not be just a matter of an apparently unitary process being broken down into a multiplicity of smaller processes. These multiple processes may be arranged vertically in a series of levels – or at least sets or series of them might be – in which higher level processes, while being constituted by lower level ones, may nevertheless have a reflex effect on the lower level ones. Also processes at one level may loop back on to themselves, and so on. In short, how intentionality is constituted at these lower levels may be very complicated indeed and there is no denying that from the viewpoint of the present it remains a genuine mystery.

Dennett has described this strategy of analysing the psychological or intentional levels of explanation into bottom-level, probably

---

and 'speech centre' in his models of consciousness and introspection. As Rorty points out, for example, the inputs and outputs of the 'analyser' are suspiciously like what was referred to by the oldfashioned mentalist term 'thoughts,' except that there is added, gratuitously, that they are now items locatable in the brain, at least in principle.

In his paper, ' "Functionalism" in Philosophy of Psychology,' in *Proceedings of the Aristotelian Society*, 80 (1979-80) 221-2, Norman Malcolm suggests that this is a symptom of a deeper problem – unavoidable circularity in explanation – inherent in this type of functionalism.

biological, explanations as a 'top-down' strategy, that is, a 'strategy that begins with a more abstract decomposition of the highest levels of psychological organisation, and hopes to analyse these into more and more detailed smaller systems or processes until finally one arrives at elements familiar to the biologists.'[31] So the functional physicalist who employs this 'top-down' strategy aims to reduce the top-layer intentional description to a bottom-level description of purely mechanistic processes for it is only at this bottom level that the psychological can be absorbed into the explanations proffered by the traditional natural sciences.

Besides admitting that this is a strategy that cannot be carried out now, Dennett also recognises that the chief difficulty in such a programme is in analysing away the first level reference to mental representation – and its companion ghost, the homunculus who understands or interprets the representation – which seems deeply embedded in our intentional descriptions. As Dennett puts it, 'Psychology *without* homunculi is impossible. But psychology *with* homunculi is doomed to circularity or infinite regress, so psychology is impossible.'[32] That is, prima facie it seems impossible to give an account of mental states such as knowing, believing, and describing without at least implicitly incorporating into the account the need for some system of mental representation. For example, to believe that it will rain tomorrow is to take up a certain attitude (of believing to be true or of holding that it is most likely to be brought about or some such) to a content (rain tomorrow), and so the content must somehow be represented *now* in the mind for the attitude in question to govern it or operate over it. Now if there is a representation (image, picture, code, icon, symbol) of something, then it seems there must be an homunculus in the brain to understand (see, interpret, decipher) it. But if you posit an homunculus in the brain as part of the explanation of how we believe or know or desire or understand, then you will have to posit another smaller homunculus within the brain of the first homunculus as part of the explanation of how the first homunculus

---

31 'Artificial intelligence as philosophy and as psychology,' *Brainstorms*, 122

32 *Ibid.*

understands, interprets or deciphers the internal representation, and so on ad infinitum.

The way out, says Dennett, is to posit 'representations that understand themselves' and the best way to achieve this is to replace the homunculi, first with a committee of 'relatively ignorant, narrow-minded, homunculi' and then to replace these committees with sub-committees of 'homunculi so stupid (all they have to do is remember whether to say yes or no when asked) that they can be, as one says, "replaced by a machine".' In general, then, says Dennett, 'one *discharges* fancy homunculi from one's scheme by organising armies of such idiots to do the work.'[33] This programme, he suggests, can be said to have been begun already by those working in artificial intelligence.[34]

However Dennett immediately grants that 'one never quite gets *completely* self-understanding representations' and that there is a danger in concluding from the success of current modest exercises in simulating, for example, human dialogue, that there is no reason to believe that in the future one can duplicate human understanding in the mechanistic subroutines of a machine.

This belief that the future will teach us how the mental can be reduced to a series of complex mechanistic processes, that loop and swirl, interlock and overlap, may turn out to be merely a pious hope. Philosophers have a distinct fondness for the concept 'future science' but, given the present paucity of genuine signposts, the present confidence in the future direction of the cognitive cum brain sciences – confidence that the future will show that the journey along the path of reductive analyses will be fruitful – may be misplaced.

Leaving aside the fact that functionalism which seeks such reductions contains a large element of promises rather than settlements, there is a far more fundamental worry about Dennett's particular programme of reducing the homunculi to zombies, for this programme runs counter to one of his own basic sources of inspiration. In major

---

33 *Brainstorms*, 123-4

34 Dennett draws attention, for example, to Winograd's SHRDLU programme in *Understanding Natural Language* (New York: Academic Press 1972).

part the point of putting forward an account of the mental in terms of intentional systems is that it avoids the eliminative materialist's difficulties in having to cope with the ever increasing likelihood that there is nothing in the brain to correspond to what in ordinary 'folk psychology' are called beliefs, desires, and intuitions. So to attempt to reduce 'folk psychological' items – whether by means of intervening stages of homunculi or not – to the mechanistic acts of zombies, is to fall back into the very eliminative materialist's difficulties which the whole functionalist approach was designed to avoid.

If Dennett were to suggest that the subroutines, to which the higher level homuncular or intentional acts are to be reduced, are not meant to be nor to mirror in any way biological processes or routines – though, as we have seen, he does say quite clearly in a number of places that this is what they are – then one is hard put to see the point of the exercise of reducing higher level, fictional, computationally-convenient routines to lower-level ones. As I've suggested above, the point may be only to *simulate* in the machines of artificial intelligence what goes on in a human's head before he or she acts, but this can have only tangential usefulness as part of the programme – psychology's programme – of explaining the nature of human mentality. The psychologist, when considering human mentality, wants to know what it is for a human to believe and desire, not how to build a machine which simulates the intervening stages between input and output in believing and desiring humans. Admittedly to find out about the latter may be instructive about some aspects of the former, for example, it might inform us whether a particular elaborated model for human mentality would produce something like human behaviour. It can be used as a test bed for certain aspects of theories of human mentality.

Even if it came about that there was a successful artificial-intelligence reduction of abstract intentional states to abstract but non-intentional subroutines, this would show that there was no a priori barrier to *an* elimination of the intentional but it would not show how to reduce human intentionality to brain processes or even whether this could be done. So, even if it sees itself as allied to the 'artificial intelligence' stance, the 'intentional system' stance is still moving a long way from psychological explanation (or, for that matter, from traditional philosophy of mind.)

In general, then, Dennett's 'case study' of introspection is very revealing of the difficulties in functionalism in psychological explanation, whether it be free-standing functionalism (which might usefully be called 'artificial intelligence functionalism') or functionalism that seeks reductions from the intentional to sub-personal, biological, mechanistic subroutines. In its most abstract free-standing form, functionalism could be said once again to have split off the psychological from the physical. The psychological or mental 'world' would be an invented world more or less wholly indifferent to the physical world.[35] The pure functionalists could be said to have invented psycho-physical lack-of-parallelism. In its reductive form, functionalism could be said to have reduced itself to eliminative materialism.[36]

Received November, 1983

---

35 Searle is interesting on this aspect of functionalism, see his 'Minds, brains, and programs,' in *The Mind's I*, esp. 371-2.

36 I would like to take the opportunity of acknowledging the award from the Nuffield Foundation of a Fellowship to pursue research into introspection and the benefit of comments on earlier drafts from my former colleague Jim Edwards.

CANADIAN JOURNAL OF PHILOSOPHY
Supplementary Volume 11

Functionalism and the Argument from Conceivability

JANET LEVIN
School of Philosophy, University of Southern California, University Park
Los Angeles, CA 90007

In recent years, functionalism has emerged as the most appealing candidate for a materialistic theory of mind. Its central thesis – that types of mental states can be defined in terms of their causal and counterfactual relations to the sensory stimulations, other internal states, and behavior of the entities that have them – offers hope for a reasonable materialism: it promises type-identity conditions for beliefs, sensations, and emotions that are not irreducibly mental, yet would permit entities that are physically quite different to be in mental states of the same type.[1]

1 The earliest leading proponents of functionalism were Putnam, Fodor, and David Lewis. Sellars and Lewis, early on, advanced proto-functionalist views

Functionalists by no means have a common understanding about what these causal and counterfactual relations will be. David Lewis, for example, asserts that any adequate functional definition of mental states must derive from common knowledge – our so-called 'common sense theory of mind,' whereas Putnam and Fodor believe that these definitions will include the 'esoterica'[2] of theoretical psychology. Still others fall somewhere in between. To many hopeful materialists, however, the dispute between the 'analytic' and the 'scientific' functionalists is a detail that need not be settled until calmer, post-revolutionary times: just as we did not need to know whether pain was in fact correlated with C-fiber stimulation in order to judge the plausibility of the identity thesis, so we may withhold judgment about the final form of functionalism. First on the agenda, and independent of these details, should be the defense of functionalism against objections which, if sound, would threaten every version of the doctrine.

And indeed, there have been many challenges to functionalism at large, particularly with regard to its prospects for defining mental states with experiential or qualitative content, states such as feeling pain, having an after-image, or seeing red.[3] The most powerful and tenacious of these challenges, in my view, depends upon what I shall call the 'argument from conceivability.' This argument begins with the claim that, for any functional description, we can imagine or conceive of a being that satisfies it, yet is unable to feel what we feel when gripped by a headache or blinded by a light. But, the argument continues,

---

as well. See Ned Block, 'Troubles With Functionalism,' in W. Savage, ed., *Minnesota Studies in the Philosophy of Science*, Vol. IX (Minneapolis: University of Minnesota Press 1978) 261-326, for a comprehensive discussion of the doctrine.

I have presented functionalism as an attempt to provide necessary and sufficient conditions for an entity to be in a mental state of a certain type. It may also be presented as a property identity thesis, e.g., the property of being in pain is identical with the property of being in a state with a certain functional role.

2 This word is David Lewis', in 'Radical Interpretation,' *Synthese*, **23** (1974) 335.

3 E.g., by Block and Fodor in 'What Psychological States are Not', *Philosophical Review*, **81** (1972), 159-81 and by Block, in 'Troubles With Functionalism.'

if we can imagine or conceive of such beings, it is possible for them to exist. Therefore, no functional description could provide necessary and sufficient conditions for an entity to be in those mental states.

Functionalism, of course, can be defended in a number of ways. One approach is to question the legitimacy of drawing conclusions about what is possible from considerations of what can be imagined or conceived. A second approach is to accept some such link between conceivability and possibility, but deny that a reasoned, reflective attempt to imagine a counterexample could actually succeed. On first glance, the latter approach may seem dubious, leading at best to an impasse between the functionalist and the dualist, while the former has the earmarks of empiricistic good sense. Nonetheless, I shall propose and endorse a strategy of the second type, and argue that it provides the *only* non-question-begging defense of the doctrine against the argument from conceivability.[4] I shall also argue that the psychophysical identity thesis cannot be defended along these lines, a conclusion that should have interest for anti-functionalists who would be materialists in some other way.

However, this strategy imposes certain constraints upon the form of functional definitions: on the one hand, they will be required to have empirical content that is not part of our common sense theory, yet they must, on the other hand, provide an explication of our ordinary mental concepts. Although, as I shall argue, these constraints are not incompatible, they demand that there be room for both 'analytic' and 'scientific' elements in a successful functionalist theory. Thus, it will not be possible to defend functionalism against the argument from conceivability without making a substantive claim about its final form.

To pursue this strategy, it will be necessary to examine the way in which the argument from conceivability is supposed to work against

4 Although I shall limit my discussion to the effect of the argument from conceivability upon a functionalist account of sensation, it can be extended to similar objections to related views, such as Searle's attack on computational theories of understanding in 'Minds, Brains, and Programs,' reprinted in J. Haugeland, ed., *Mind Design* (Cambridge, MA: Bradford Books 1981) 282-306.

functionalism, and then to look critically at the ground of the argument itself. Let us test our intuitions, then, on the following case.

I. Imagining a Person who Cannot Feel Pain

This case involves a being who, at least initially, is by hypothesis unable to feel any pain. It is significant that this thought-experiment involves a *human* being, and not a computer-driven robot or a creature composed of homunculi that play the roles of neurons,[5] but I believe that if we get clear about what can be conceived or imagined in the case of humans, the others will also fall into place.

Consider, then, a person, Jones, born without the capacity to feel pain.[6] There are living examples of this affliction; as might be expected, they must be carefully monitored, as they can break bones, suffer burns, and develop internal injuries without being aware of it. So far, this provides no problem for the functionalist; though these people are not in pain, they are also not in states with the appropriate functional roles. However, in order for them to have the least chance of survival, such people have to learn to notice their bodily states and judge that they are in injurious circumstances, and do their best to avoid similar circumstances at the time and in the future.

Let us imagine, then, that Jones is explicitly taught the signs and consequences of impending bodily injury by receiving rules such as the following: 'When your hand is sufficiently close to a flame, you are in a state that you should seek to get out of (since it leads to bodily damage), and by withdrawing your hand you will get out of it.' Once the lessons were firmly entrenched, Jones will come to believe, when his hand is sufficiently close to a flame, that he is in a state that he

5 As, for example, Block's case of the population of China which duplicates his functional organization for an hour, in 'Troubles With Functionalism,' in Savage, 279.

6 An account of this phenomenon is given in R. Melzack, *The Puzzle of Pain* (New York: Basic Books 1973) 15-16.

prefers not to be in, which is similar to and different from various of his other bodily states. Further, he will desire to be out of that state, and will take every step to remove himself from the situation. Have we now imagined a being that satisfies the functional definition of 'pain' without feeling pain?

It seems not, upon reflection. What we have imagined here is merely the case of a person who is in a state that has some of the typical effects of the state we are in when in pain. It is easy, however, to point to differences in the roles of those states. For example, normal pain feelers must have an unconditional or underived dislike of the state that satisfies the functional definition of 'pain': it is part of the functional role of pain to produce the unconditional desire to remove oneself from that state. (The desire, of course, is sometimes overridden by others, but its production is nevertheless part of the functional role of pain.) In Jones' case, however, his desire to remove himself from the 'painful' circumstances is highly derived; his aversion to the state is conditional upon his knowledge of its typical consequences.

However, we can revise the example to insure that Jones does have the right underived desires. Such a person can indeed be imagined to have an intrinsic, and not merely conditional, dislike of such a state, compatible with our hypothesis that he feels no pain. If the lessons are well enough learned, he may develop a habitual aversion, which, though initially caused by his knowledge of the usual consequences of that state, automatically attaches to the state itself. Would *this* be a case of a person who satisfies the functional definition of 'pain' without feeling pain?

No, or not yet, at any rate. Even though Jones' 'pain' states produced the same beliefs, desires, and behavior as ours, there is nevertheless a difference in their respective causes. For him, it will be neither bodily injury itself, nor the stimulation of any sensory receptors, that produces the state which in turn gives rise to the relevant beliefs and desires, but the *threat* of injury, or the attention paid to situations that would *seem* injurious, that is causally relevant. Our pain states, but not his 'pain' states, would produce the relevant beliefs and desires in us even at times at which we were not paying attention to the part of the body that is, or is about to be, afflicted. Thus there is a functional difference between our state of pain and the state responsible for such beliefs and desires in a person who, by hypothesis, cannot feel pain.

But the example can be developed further still. Suppose that we set Jones up with a monitoring device which would, in appropriate circumstances, automatically put him into the state that gives rise to all the beliefs and desires, and all the avoidance behavior, associated with pain in us. This device, perhaps an implant into the brain (or the brain and the sensory receptors), would be activated by just the same environmental stimuli that elicit pain in us; it could operate, at least in certain cases, when Jones was distracted, inattentive, or asleep. Further, just as in our case, it could even be set off sometimes by internal occurrences that do not herald impending injury at all. In short, this device would permit Jones to be in a state that had exactly the functional role of pain. Haven't we now, finally, imagined a person who satisfies the functional definition of 'pain' without feeling pain? Here a dualist might get impatient, and ask what more the functionalist could want!

But the functionalist could agree that *if* Jones were implanted with such a device, and were nonetheless unable to feel pain, then there would be trouble for the doctrine. He could deny, however, that this is what the dualist has actually imagined. Just as in the earlier stages of the story of Jones, what has been imagined here is a being who satisfies merely some approximation of the functional definition of 'pain.' In thinking about Jones at this latest stage, it would have been easy for the dualist to have overlooked certain elements of the functional role of pain, and thus not to have conceived of a being that is functionally like us at all. Even in the earlier stages of the story, we saw that the functional role of pain was quite complex, and that some of its features came to mind only after considerable reflection. Further, it is most likely that there are causes and effects of pain that we do not even know about, that only future empirical investigation will uncover. If so, then even the ideally attentive imaginer may not be in a position, now, to properly imagine a person who is in a state functionally equivalent to pain. For a dualist, then, to claim that he has imagined such a state would be overconfident at best. Indeed, the functionalist can go further and claim that as we add details to our picture of Jones after his operation, it will become increasingly unnatural to regard him as a non-pain-feeler; we will be tempted to conclude that the operation has given Jones the capacity to feel pain for the first time.

It may seem that we have now reached the impasse to which my strategy had threatened to lead. The dualist has claimed to have imagined a counterexample to a functionalist account of sensation, and the functionalist has provided an alternative explanation of what has been imagined. But how is this exchange of intuitions to be evaluated?

It is time, then, to look closely at the role of conceivability in metaphysical argument, and even more important, to address the question of why a good materialistic functionalist needs to take conceivability arguments seriously in the first place. Why not simply reject the claim that what we can conceive of or imagine has any bearing on what can or cannot be?

II. What is the Argument from Conceivability, and Why Should it be Taken Seriously?

Though arguments that proceed from the imaginability of a situation to its possibility were common among the early modern philosophers, they have recently been viewed with some suspicion. It is easy to see why: after all, people vary greatly in their imaginative abilities, and some even claim to be able to imagine situations that we firmly believe to be impossible. However, these arguments have again begun to command attention, and have been used with increasing frequency against various forms of materialism. It is Kripke who has set the example. In 'Naming and Necessity' he helped to describe and reinforce the evidential link between imaginability and possibility by showing how various claims to have imagined the impossible can be successfully explained away.[7] Further, he used this sort of argument to great effect against the psycho-physical identity thesis. In this section, I shall borrow loosely from Kripke's discussion, and some remarks of W.D. Hart, in attempting to say when claims to have imagined or conceived of a situation shed light upon its possibility. I shall try to preserve the

7 In D. Davidson and G. Harman, eds., *Semantics of Natural Language* (Boston, MA: D. Reidel 1972) 253-355.

spirit, if not the letter, of their discussions, though I may differ with them in the ultimate evaluation of what conceivability has to do with the metaphysics of mental states.

Clearly, no account of conceivability can warrant any claim to have imagined a situation which cannot be described without flouting the rules of first-order logic. But any plausible account of conceivability will also have to rule out various claims to have imagined situations which can be described without (first-order) contradiction. For example, we would want to dismiss claims to have discovered that there is a procedure for squaring the circle, or that there is a mechanical procedure for generating all and only the arithmetical truths, where these claims result from inattention to a crucial lack of clarity or completeness in the procedures one has in mind. Also, we must rule out cases in which someone clearly imagines, say, a Euclidean triangle, and claims that its angles do not add up to 180 degrees. Here the triangle may have been clearly pictured, but certain obvious consequences of its being a triangle have not been noticed.

These claims, it seems, arise because the imaginer has taken the proposition in question to describe a situation that is not clearly in focus, the details of which he has not adequately surveyed. I do not want to rest too much weight upon the details of this diagnosis, on pain of straining the metaphor of imagination as the scrutiny of mental images. Nonetheless, I shall encapsulate what is wrong with these claims by saying that the situations they purport to describe are not *clearly and distinctly imagined or conceived*.[8]

There are other cases, however, which cannot be handled in this way, cases which Kripke has labelled the a posteriori necessary truths. For example, it is sometimes claimed, on the strength of what can be imagined, that temperature could have been distinct from mean kinetic energy. But for Kripke, the proposition that temperature is

---

8 In what follows, I shall be speaking indifferently of imaginability and conceivability, and will not attempt to distinguish the two. Some interesting remarks on this subject are made by W.D. Hart in 'Imagination, Necessity, and Abstract Objects,' in M. Schirn, ed., *Studies on Frege*, Vol. 1 (Stuttgart, Germany: Frommann-Holzboog 1976) 161-92, in which he denies that we can imagine relations among abstract entities. But I shall not comment upon them here.

mean kinetic energy is, if true, a necessary truth.[9] How, then, can the apparent conceivability of its denial be explained away? After all, it seems as if we could easily imagine a world in which we felt warmth only upon contact with x-rays, and cold only upon contact with gamma rays, and thus a world in which temperature and mean kinetic energy were distinct. Our ability to imagine such a world, however, does not arise from inattention to any vagueness or incompleteness in what has actually been imagined.

Kripke, however, marshals a different set of considerations in explaining away these claims. What we have here, says Kripke, is not a vagueness or incompleteness in the scenario imagined, but a different kind of mismatch between what has been imagined and how it has been described. What has really been imagined is not a world in which temperature is distinct from mean kinetic energy, but a world in which the *sensations* that temperature produces in this world are produced by something else. We might misdescribe that world initially because we unreflectively take 'temperature' to refer to whatever in that world produces sensations of heat and cold, but further reflection leads us to recognize that, given the way we use the word 'temperature,' it refers to the same thing in every possible world, namely, the physical phenomenon that produces sensations of temperature in ours. However, though 'temperature' does not mean the same as 'phenomenon that produces sensations of heat and cold,' the phrases are commonly associated. This explains how we could have mistaken the world we have actually imagined for one in which temperature and mean kinetic energy were distinct, and the change of mind that we have upon reflection allows this explanation to stand.

Thus, even though a scenario is clearly and distinctly conceived, further reflection may cause us to reject a certain description of it. This will be legitimate as long as it is possible for the imaginer to have mistaken the occurrence of the actual-world effects of the phenomenon in question for the occurrence of the phenomenon itself, and as long as the imaginer agrees, upon reflection, that this is a plausible explanation of his initial response.

---

9 In what follows, I shall assume without discussion that Kripke's account of the semantics of natural kind terms is correct.

Now, one might think that this strategy could be used against the dualist who claims to have imagined pain in the absence of C-fiber stimulation, as the proposition that pain is identical with the firing of C-fibers would, if true, be an a posteriori necessary truth. But, according to Kripke, there is a crucial difference between this case and the identity of temperature and mean kinetic energy. Just as in that case, we can construct a scenario that appears to be clearly and distinctly conceived: for example, a situation in which we feel headachy, but notice no C-fiber stimulation on our cerebroscopes. So if the identity thesis is true, we should be able to give an alternative description of what has been imagined, and explain how it could have been mistaken for a world in which pain was distinct from C-fiber stimulation. But here, according to Kripke, is where the analogy breaks down: whereas there could be a world in which something other than mean kinetic energy felt like temperature to perceivers, any phenomenon that felt like pain to perceivers would just *be* pain. Thus, there will be no hope of explaining away the imagined scenario as a world that merely seems to be, but is not really, a world in which pain and C-fiber stimulation were distinct.

Since 'Naming and Necessity,' however, it has been argued that Kripke's strategy for dismissing the apparent contingency of 'Temperature is mean kinetic energy' can indeed be extended to the claims of the identity theorist. Putnam and Boyd, for example,[10] have argued that all that is required is the existence of a criterial but contingent description associated with *one or the other* of the terms in the identity statement. It is not necessary to find a description so associated with 'pain' as long as there is one so associated with 'C-fiber stimulation.' And there is, namely, 'the state that our instruments (usually) report as C-fiber stimulation.' In a world in which our instruments were defective, this description might denote the secretion of adrenalin, or the firing of the optic nerve. But if so, then what we have imagined can be redescribed as a world in which we are mistaken

---

10 As reported in Block's 'Troubles With Functionalism,' in Savage, 287. See also Boyd's 'Materialism Without Reduction,' 84, in N. Block, ed., *Readings in the Philosophy of Psychology*, Vol. I (Cambridge, MA: Harvard 1981).

about whether our C-fibers have been stimulated, and thus falsely believe that C-fiber stimulation can occur in the absence of pain.

Is it plausible, though, that this is what has been imagined? Unfortunately, the mere existence of an alternative explanation would not yet vindicate the identity theorist; what would be required is an explanation that is intuitively acceptable, indeed preferable, to the imaginer. But most people, including many who would be materialists, resist the claim that what they have imagined is a world in which, though pain really is identical with C-fiber stimulation, the best available instruments for detecting such a correlation invariably lead us to mistake.

There have been a number of explanations of why this redescription does not soothe the intuitions. For example, Ned Block criticizes this explanation because it depends essentially on the invocation of widespread mistake.[11] I do not think it is mistakenness per se that makes this explanation unsatisfactory, but the rather implausible implication that we would not be able to imagine a similar scenario in which our instruments *were* reliable, but nevertheless reported C-fiber stimulation in the absence of pain. In any case, we need not dwell upon why this explanation is unsatisfactory now. Nothing in this discussion so far, or in anything Kripke says, requires that our intuitions about the adequacy of an alternative explanation be justified or explained. The very existence of these intuitions gives prima facie weight to the claim that pain could exist without C-fiber stimulation, and thus that the identity thesis is false.

It is here that many materialists may be tempted to reject the argument from conceivability, and complain that it is grounded in a vicious circle. After all, a proposition will count as conceivable if we can imagine what we take to be a world in which it is true, and no further reflection shakes the faith that we have indeed imagined such a world. But our judgments about whether we have imagined such a world depend upon our judgments about whether such a world *can* be imagined, and these, in turn, upon judgments about whether such a world is possible. So, to take the conceivability of a proposition P as

11 In 'Troubles With Functionalism,' Savage, 287.

evidence of its possibility is just to say 'You should believe P to be possible only if you *really think* it is possible,' and provides, at best, a way of systematizing the beliefs about P's possibility that we already had. Thus it is illegitimate to treat considerations about what can be imagined as providing insight into what is possible.

I think that these observations are correct, but that the conclusion does not follow. It is true that our judgments about whether a description of an imagined situation is mistaken are based upon all sorts of considerations – intuition, uncontested background beliefs, current theories, common sense – and that our determination of whether we can really conceive of a situation serve primarily to bring all these to bear. But this is just the evidence that ought, and all the evidence that could, be brought to bear at this time upon the possibility of a proposition. Further, considerations such as these have been important tools for philosophers of all sympathies, and *especially* for functionalists. After all, it is usually from considerations of what can be conceived or imagined that the functionalist, as well as the dualist, argues that the type-identity thesis is incorrect. Thus, though our beliefs about the possibility of any proposition are revisable in light of new evidence, or shifts in intuition, we are justified now in believing P to be possible if we have clearly and distinctly imagined a scenario that seems, after due reflection, to be best described by P. At the very least, a rather heavy burden of proof will be shifted to the person who claims that P is not possible.[12]

To be sure, there is room for the identity theorist to ask for time: to claim that all the evidence is not in, or that his opponent is saddled with intuitions that will change with the growth of knowledge. Both these claims may well be true, but we have no particular reason to believe them now. The functionalist, however, is in a much stronger position, or so I will argue, as reflection upon the story of Jones will show.

---

12 This view about conceivability owes much to conversations with Tamara Horowitz.

III. Conceivability and Explication

What, then, is the bearing of the discussion of conceivability on the case of Jones? First, I hope I have made a case for the legitimacy, in metaphysical arguments, of considered intuitions about what can be imagined or conceived. Second, I hope I have provided a structure within which we can evaluate specific claims to have imagined or conceived of a certain situation, in particular, the claim that Jones, in his final state, embodied a counterexample to functionalism.

In my previous discussion, I suggested that any such claim would be mistaken: either the imaginer had failed to consider, or was completely unaware of, some crucial part of the relevant functional definition. But is this plausible, especially in light of my remarks about the strategy used by Putnam and Boyd in their unsatisfying defense of the identity thesis? Just as they claimed we are mistaken in thinking we had imagined a being with C-fiber stimulation, I claim that we are mistaken in thinking that we had imagined a being in a state with a certain functional role. How can their strategy be implausible, and mine not? A closer look, however, will reveal differences in our lines of defense.

Putnam and Boyd acknowledge that we could imagine, in as great detail as we like, a scenario in which our cerebroscopes report C-fiber stimulation in the absence of pain. Though this may seem to be a world in which pain and C-fiber stimulation are distinct, they argue that it can be redescribed as a world in which faulty cerebroscopes always lead us to mistake. On my explanation, however, our being mistaken is not part of the content of what has been imagined, but is a feature of our condition here in the actual world: our actual ignorance of, or failure to attend to, the details of the functional role of pain encourages us to think, incorrectly, that we have imagined someone functionally like us who does not feel pain.

Unlike Putnam and Boyd, I do not need to find a criterial but contingent description associated either with 'pain' or its functional description. This is because, unlike them, I did not use Kripke's strategy for explaining away the intuition that temperature might not have been mean kinetic energy. Rather than argue that the denial of the functional definition of 'pain' is a mistaken description of a clearly imagined but entirely different situation, I have claimed that the scenario that was to stand witness for the possibility of the proposition has not been clearly and distinctly conceived. Further, I suggested a natural explanation of how this mistake could have been made, one that appealed to the dynamics of the attempt to imagine a counter-example to functionalism that emerged from the story of Jones.

But have I merely traded one implausibility for another? It is clear that my explanation is modelled not upon Kripke's account of why it seems that temperature might not have been mean kinetic energy, but upon his (and Hart's) account of the apparent conceivability of the denials of mathematical and geometrical truths. This suggests that the functional definition of 'pain' must provide some sort of explication of our ordinary concept, since my account commits me to the claim that if omniscient, ideally attentive imaginers had the functional role of pain clearly in mind, they would find it *inconceivable* for a being to be in a state with that role and feel no pain. But is it plausible to think that any functional definition of 'pain' could have this status? And if it is, how could this be reconciled with my earlier claim that the correct functional definition of 'pain' need not draw information solely from our common sense beliefs about that phenomenon, but may include information uncovered by psychological investigation as well? As well as being independently attractive, this claim was crucial to my explanation of what was being imagined by the dualist in the final stage of the story of Jones.

In response to the second question, it does indeed follow from my view that a satisfactory functional definition of 'pain' must in some sense provide an explication of our ordinary concept. But the development of an explicative definition can be sensitive to empirical findings nonetheless. A good explication will, among other things, preserve intuitions about which objects (and possible objects) fall under the concept in question. It will provide metaphysically necessary and sufficient conditions for when an object is an object of the relevant kind. Now, empirical considerations have two distinct roles to play in the development and revision of such necessary and sufficient conditions. First, we might revise an explicative definition upon confrontation with an object that meets the conditions, but does not seem, intuitively, to fall under the concept in question. This could lead us to complicate the definition so as to rule this sort of object out. Such a discovery would provide data that, by sharpening our intuitions, would force us to modify our definitions. Yet these objects might be so unlike anything we have so far seen or imagined that we would not, in their absence, have been able to make the required imaginative leap.

As an example, consider a definition that once (could have) counted as an explication of 'free action,' namely, 'action performed without external compulsion.' Though the empirical observation of the discrepancy between the avowals and the behavior of a kleptomaniac might have led us to a theory in light of which we revised this definition, this observation would have called our attention to a counterexample that could have been constructed by a thought-experiment alone. Consider even a mathematical example such as Church's Thesis, in which the well-understood concept of recursiveness serves to explicate the less precise, intuitive concept of effective computability. Even this identity could be disconfirmed by what look to be empirical considerations: if we discovered a machine that effectively computed functions according to an algorithm for which there was no recursive definition, we would have found an empirical counterexample to Church's Thesis. Here again, the empirical discovery would have served to alert us to a possibility that had been there all along, yet it would have been extremely important if it helped to direct our limited imaginations to defects in the explications at hand.

There is another, perhaps more important, role for empirical investigation in the refinement of an explicative definition. We may discover entities that fit our current definition without seeming to fall under the concept in question, yet we may not, as of now, be able to see how they can be justifiably ruled out. It may require long and close observation of these beings, and the construction of a theory that explains those observations, to uncover the relevant differences between entities that are, and those that are not, of that kind. Again, consider kleptomania, and the trouble it makes for a definition of 'free action.' Though the mere observation of a kleptomaniac's behavior may alert us to the deficiency of our definition, we may not be able to revise it until we have more of a general theory of compulsive behavior. Such a theory, moreover, may not be forthcoming until observations of other behavioral anomalies have been made. Nonetheless, our definition of 'free action' may still count as explicative of that concept. Similarly, though one might not call this discovery 'empirical,' the proper explication of effective computability had to await the discovery of the class of general recursive functions. In both these cases, however, the role of empirical investigation and theory construction is primarily suggestive – it serves to provide resources for the expression of conditions that will be, when understood, intuitively adequate as explications of the concepts in question. Thus a functionalist who assumes that further study of the causes and effects of pain in human beings may be necessary to enable us to identify just what it is that differentiates us from those that seem incapable of feeling pain need not be giving up the project of explication.

Indeed, analytic functionalists ought to welcome, rather than resist, (at least some) help from the empirical psychologists. If their aim is to make explicit our common sense theory of mind, it should be remembered that this body of beliefs is supposed to be a *theory*, albeit one that embodies information that we commonly hold. It would be unfortunate to restrict the content of common sense theory to what is *now* considered common property, as this would rule out the possibility of theoretical growth and change. Further, it would belie the actual histories of common sense theories, since we see frequent examples, from folk medicine to popular psychology, of the incorporation into 'common sense' of initially esoteric information about the items involved. Just how much theory and empirical discovery can be incorporated into an alleged explication without changing the subject will be left an open question here. I want to argue merely that such theory and discovery is compatible with explication and common sense.

But even if I am correct about the role of observation and theory construction in explication, one might wonder whether *any* functional definition, even the best-known platitudes about the subject, could possibly provide an explication of pain.

One source of worry may be the fear that no amount of knowledge of the functional role of pain could reveal what pain is *like* to a person who had never felt it.[13] Indeed, it may be doubted that the full descrip-

---

13 As stated in T. Nagel, 'What is it Like to be a Bat?', *Philosophical Review* **83** (October 1974) 435-50.

tion of the functional role of pain would suggest the relevant experience even to a person who had felt pain. Ultimately, the functionalist will have to address this sort of objection, but its merits and deficiencies are not relevant to the argument from conceivability. The inconceivability in which I am interested does not require that the thought of how pain feels spring to mind immediately, or ever, upon contemplation of its functional role. Otherwise, given that we can imagine a cube without immediately, or ever, thinking of a figure with twelve edges, we would count as being able to clearly and distinctly imagine a cube that is not a twelve-edged figure. Rather, I am claiming that if we think carefully about a human being in a state with that role, and think about the way pain feels, we will not be tempted to think we had imagined a being who did not feel like *that*.

Another worry may be that I have focussed exclusively upon a third-person case, the case of Jones, whereas the real test of the dualist's intuitions about conceivability would be whether we can imagine *ourselves* to be in the functional state associated with pain without feeling pain. Again, I think that a full treatment of the problem of subjective experience would have to focus more closely upon the first-person case. But this will not be necessary for a satisfactory response to the argument from conceivability, as conceivability arguments in the first-person case are double-edged. Because of our familiarity with our experiential states and their causal roles, it is even harder to imagine *ourselves* as having the beliefs and underived desires we know to be caused only by pain, without having that familiar feeling. The move to the third-person case helps, rather than hinders the dualist, as it forestalls any confusion of metaphysical with psychological blocks to the imagination.

Nevertheless, my inconceivability claim may still seem suspicious. After all, the terms 'pain' and 'state with functional role R' will express different concepts, no matter how the characterization of pain is developed and refined. Further, unlike truths such as 'A cube is a solid with twelve equal edges,' which also consists of different concepts, the functional definition of 'pain' will not be provable by a priori principles such as the laws of geometry. One might wonder, then, what would stand in the way of our clearly imagining (what appeared to be) a person in such a state who felt no pain.

Classically, however, explications are judged by how well they satisfy our intuitions about which objects fall into a certain class. Even in mathematics there are explicative identities established in this way. Church's Thesis, for example, is not provable, but is supported inductively by showing that every effectively computable function so far examined has indeed been recursive. Thus, to raise this objection against functionalism is to dig in one's heels and claim that there just cannot be an explication of pain in functionalist terms – that a counterexample to any definition can always be constructed. This conviction, however, requires argument, and I suspect that such an argument would be extremely difficult to press.

Yet though I have argued that a suitably empirical functional definition *could* be explicative, I have not yet argued that it *will* be. How can I be confident that the denial of the ultimate functional definition of 'pain' will be inconceivable, especially given that we may not yet have the correct definition in hand? I see evidence, however, in the development of the story of Jones, evidence which, moreover, is not available to an identity theorist who might wish to make a similar claim.

I began the story by noting a significant difference between Jones and ourselves, namely, that Jones was incapable of feeling pain. In the successive stages of the story, I attempted to diminish the difference by giving him more and more of the capacity to function like us. Each time, however, until perhaps the last, it became obvious that functional differences remained. Now, two interesting things emerge from these considerations. First, it is clear that once we thought hard about each stage of Jones' transformation, we realized that he did not satisfy the correct functional definition, though we may have thought so at first glance. That is, once we had clearly and distinctly grasped what state Jones was in, we knew that the state was not pain, and we knew why. Now I believe that the only plausible account of this dual conviction is that, in each case, our clarity about Jones' state led us to identify a functional difference between Jones and ourselves. This claim is controversial, of course, and may be taken to beg the question. Thus I shall not insist upon any particular explanation of this conviction, but will note merely that, at each stage, our recognition of Jones' continued incapacity, whatever its source, drew our attention to various features of the role of pain that had until then escaped our notice. It put us in mind of certain commonly known facts about the causes and effects of pain which we could incorporate into better and better versions of our definition. So far, then, the development of the story of Jones involved a procedure very much like the revision of an explicative definition in the face of threatened counterexample.

What, then, about the final stage in the story of Jones? As I have argued, we have not clearly and distinctly imagined a being who is functionally like us but incapable of feeling pain, because we have not clearly and distinctly imagined someone who satisfied the full and accurate functional definition of 'pain.' If we could somehow recapture the content of what it was that we did imagine, and get clear about its details, we may well be able to consult our implicit common sense beliefs about pain to once again see what we had left out. But even if not, that would not end the matter. As I have suggested before, it is not likely that current common sense alone encapsulates sufficient information about pain to distinguish Jones from a normal pain feeler. Further empirical discoveries may be required to identify the functional differences between them, and only then could we get closer to the correct functional definition of 'pain.' The need for such empirical input, however, would be perfectly compatible with the explicative nature of the definition.

A similar story can be told, I believe, for cases that may initially seem harder. It might be thought that the difficulties for functionalism become more striking when we try to imagine computer-driven robots or homunculi-headed creatures that are functionally like us, for these creatures seem not to be sentient at all. But here, too, I would urge a re-examination of these intuitions. Like Lycan and Dennett, and other philosophers who have addressed these cases, I would argue that we have not yet come close to imagining what these beings would have to be like in order for them to duplicate even a crude approximation of our functional organization.[14] As these philosophers suggest, the scale of these creatures, and in the case of homunculi-heads, their recognizably human components, prevent our imaginations from taking hold. I endorse these explanations of why these cases do not count

---

14 E.g., W.G. Lycan, in 'Form, Function, and Feel,' *Journal of Philosophy* 78 (January 1981) 24-50, and Dennett, in conversation.

as counterexamples to functionalism, and would predict that if we had a better grasp of the internal structure and behavior of any creature that was actually functionally like us, then our intuition that it could not be sentient would pale.

Of course, the ultimate vindication of functionalism must await the development of psychological theories that provide a comprehensive account of the functional role of pain. And of course, it might be the case that we could clearly and distinctly imagine a being in just that state who could not feel pain. If so, then if we took conceivability arguments seriously, the functionalist would have to join the identity theorist in explaining away these intuitions as just so much Cartesian baggage. What I have argued here is that the functionalist is in a much stronger position than the identity theorist in explaining away any intuitions that a counterexample to the doctrine can be imagined or conceived. To be sure, my argument extracts something of a price from the functionalist, as it has implications about the nature of an adequate functional definition of mental states. As I have argued, however, the price is unavoidable, and it is not too steep for a reasonable functionalist to bear.[15]

Received February, 1983
Revised May, 1983

---

15 I am indebted to Hartry Field for extensive discussions of these issues and comments on earlier drafts of this paper. I also thank Ned Block, Barbara Herman, Brian Loar, Thomas Ricketts, and Stephen Schiffer for extremely helpful comments on various earlier drafts.

CANADIAN JOURNAL OF PHILOSOPHY
Supplementary Volume 11

A Materialist's Misgivings About Eliminative Materialism

JEFFREY FOSS
University of Victoria
Victoria, BC
V8W 2Y2

I. Introduction

I'm a materialist, and not *too* embarassed about it. It would be nice to have a knock down argument to defend materialism, but not having one, I instinctively fight off idealists, dualists, skeptics, or whatever, with the same punches and feints used by materialists from time immemorial. Like, say, the snide observation that a material like liquor gets even my idealist friends drunk, or that the senile dualists I have known don't seem at all to consist of ageless minds trapped in aging bodies. I will not resort to *ad baculum*, because all non-materialists I've known, of whatever stripe, act as though tampering with their bodies is the same as tampering with their very selves. Of course they're right to identify body and self (though they'd never admit it), so all ways of making up a person's mind require the use of physical force. But the only *proper* physical force which may be appealed to in helping someone to make up her brain is that of sound waves shaking her eardrums, or radiations from print darkening her retina. Thus (self-)restricted in my methods, there is plenty of room for embarassment when my antagonists, a brainy bunch, get round to poking at the bald spots in my materialism, asking pointed questions about sensations, thoughts, raw-feels, after-images, and so on.

This explains why I *was* so happy for the relief promised me by the new breed of materialist, the eliminative materialist. Whereas I had always felt obliged to take the position that pains, thoughts, desires, and so on, were physical things – which seemed to require the contortions necessary to pulling the very terms which I used out of my vocabulary even as I used them,[1] the eliminative materialist advised me that I could simply deny there are any such things as pains, thoughts, desires, and so on. There are no such things, whether mental *or* physical. The effect was marvellous. I really caught my old adversaries off balance. But, alas, temporary successes aside, I'm beginning to feel more like a gambler than a philosopher, betting heavily on the success of eliminative neuroscience in time to pay off

---

1 If I admitted, e.g., the existence of a red after-image, then because 'red' is not part of the proper vocabulary of physics, I had to explain the redness of the image while restricting myself to the vocabulary of physics. In other words, redness had to be *reduced* to physics. Thus materialists face the problem confronting anyone attempting an intertheoretic reduction, the problem denoted by the word 'incommensurability.' Materialistic reductions involve using terms such as 'red,' which terms must have been made to disappear or fit to disappear before the reduction is to be counted a success. It should be pointed out that though incommensurability is a thorny problem for reductions in general, it does not amount to logical inconsistency or incompatibility, and thus does not prove reductions impossible in general. Intertheoretic mappings need not be neat, one-one, or even one-many, linkages of concepts via 'bridge-laws,' along with linkages of things via transtheoretic identities. Instead, the reducing theory must be able to generate a potent image of the reduced theory with respect to the latter's domain. This is spelled out in much more detail by C.A. Hooker in his 'Towards A General Theory Of Reduction,' Parts I, II, and III, *Dialogue* **20** (1981): 38-59, 201-36, 496-529.

my anti-materialist creditors. What philosophic scruples I haven't yet wagered bid me to explain to you my gradual realization that eliminative materialism is promisory-note philosophy, and to share with you my discomfort in having been forced into prophecy in the defence of my philosophy.

It should not be thought that in criticizing eliminative materialism that I am thereby taking aim at some philosopher. For it is plain that there are no unabashed, unqualified, eliminative materialists in circulation. Rorty[2] and Hiley[3] aver that Feyerabend is an eliminative materialist – however, Feyerabend's only avowal along these lines occurs in a two page comment, 'Mental Events and the Brain,' where he says of the materialist,

> the proper procedure for him to adopt is to develop his theory without recourse to existent terminology

where by 'existent terminology' he means such as 'thought,' 'belief,' 'raw-feel,' & c[4]. However, to advise a heading for the materialist is not to set one's own course, much less to make the journey. Rorty says that Quine is an eliminative materialist, and indeed there is reason for saying so. Over thirty years ago, Quine wrote 'On Mental Entities,' in which he straightforwardly casts doubt on the whole conceptual

---

2 Richard Rorty, *Philosophy and the Mirror of Nature*, (Princeton, NJ: Princeton University Press, 1979) 117

3 David R. Hiley, 'Is Eliminative Materialism Materialistic?,' *Philosophy and Phenomenological Research* 38 (1977-78), 327

4 Paul K. Feyerabend, 'Comment: Mental Events and the Brain,' *Journal of Philosophy* 60 (1963) 295. Feyerabend does argue strongly for materialism in 'Materialism and the Mind Body Problem,' *Review of Metaphysics* 65 (1963):49-66, without, however, espousing eliminative materialism. His work there is the demolition of certain (then popular) objections to materialism, but with methods quite independent of eliminative materialism. In 'An Attempt at a Realist Interpretation of Experience,' *Proceedings of the Aristotelian Society*, 1957-8, new series, he makes some cursory comments on pp. 164-5 which may be seen as precursors to eliminative materialism, but not as eliminativism as such.

scheme of which mental entities form part of the ontology[5]. However, eight years later, when he wrote *Word and Object,* he argues very clearly towards the conclusion that there really is no difference between eliminative and reductive materialism, adding that this should not be taken as cause for alarm, but cause for rejoicing[6]:

> Some may therefore find comfort in reflecting that the distinction between an eliminative and an explicative physicalism is unreal.

Some may. Rorty's own philosophical development retraced Quine's path in roughly twice the time it took Quine to first travel the route. In 1965 Rorty published an eliminative thesis in 'Mind-Body Identity, Privacy, and Categories'[7]. By 1979, however, he said in *Philosophy and the Mirror of Nature,*

> I do not think that "eliminative materialism" is a more plausible version of the thesis of mind-brain identity than "reductive materialism." (118)
> Rather, they should both be abandoned, and with them the notion of "mind-body identity." (119)

Just in case this sounds like throwing out the baby with the bath water, Rorty offers an explanation of why such 'metaphysical' questions are otiose:

> [Such a question] is pointless not just because nobody has any idea how to resolve the issue, but because nothing turns on it. The suggestion that it *has* a clear-cut answer depends upon the pre-Quinean notion of "necessary and sufficient conditions built into our language" for the application of the terms "sensation," "mental," and the like, or upon some similar essentialism.

---

5 W.V. Quine, 'On Mental Entities' (1952), reprinted in *The Ways of Paradox* (New York: Random House 1966) 208-15

6 W.V. Quine, *Word and Object* (Cambridge, Massacusetts: M.I.T. Press 1960, 256

7 Richard Rorty, 'Mind-Body Identity, Privacy, and Categories', *Review of Metaphysics,* 19 (1965): 25-54

Both Quine and Rorty believe that the question of whether eliminative rather than reductive materialism is right (or plausible) comes down to a question concerning the anticipated development of science: will a more advanced science have any need for, or even any accomodation of, the mental? Both conclude that a more advanced neuroscience will completely map the same domain as the mental, and so will have no need of it. Moreover, they think mentalist theory so ill-defined that the question of its accomodation within science (that is, its reduction to neuroscience) is too ambiguous to require or permit an answer. To quote Rorty,

> Only a philosopher with a lot invested in the notion of "ontological status" would need to worry about whether a corrigibly reported pain was "really" a pain or rather a stimulated C-fibre.[8]

It is not surprising that when Rorty dons his anti-metaphysicalism he would, like Quine when sporting his ontological relativism, end up eschewing the question about which materialist thesis is correct. To less subtle thinkers (even post-Quinean ones who have no illusions about necessary and sufficient conditions built into our language), there seems to be a world of difference between saying that thoughts (e.g.) are made up of matter, or else saying that there are no thoughts at all. Either (virtually) all we say about the workings of each other's minds is not just an elaborate fiction, or else it is. Eschew metaphysics until your jaws ache, be as ontologically relativistic as you like, and there still remains the question of whether thoughts (and other mental things) are on a par with witches and unicorns, or on a par with tables and molecules. This is not the place to argue the merits of the coarser, pro-ontological view against the subtler anti-ontological views – and anyhow, I wouldn't know where to begin. This essay is addressed, therefore, to those who percieve the difference between the ontological status of Huck Finn and Bertrand Russell, i.e., to those who distinguish the ontologies of eliminative from reductive materialism.

---

8 Rorty, *Philosophy and the Mirror of Nature*, 120-1. Here Rorty is concerned with corrigible reports of pain (or whatever), though the point he is trying to make concerning ontology is quite general, and would apply to incorrigible reports as well, should there be such.

For Quine and Rorty, the question whether either of reductive or eliminative materialism is correct, boils down to a question of the future course of science. But note that to boil down the question this way is misleading. For one thing, nobody appeals to estimates of the *actual* course science *will* follow. No one wonders, for example, if political control of science funding might not skew results in neurophysiology. What is being appealed to instead is some *proper or preferred* course of an *ideal* truth-seeking and truth-finding science. The business of arguing whether a future (and presumably better) science will accomodate an ontology which includes thoughts (e.g.) is exactly the same business as arguing that there are thoughts. The reference to the future course of science is sometimes less than helpful, sometimes obfuscatory. Surely you can predict the future course of a *proper* science only by appealing to what you think is right now scientifically proper. So Quine's and Rorty's fence-sitting can seem contrived, to the unsubtle, since both are avowed materialists, and since both lay serious charges against the mental, hinting of its possible banishment from science altogether — all the while abstaining from calling the whole idea of the mental a mistake, fiction, falsehood, or wrong. If they do not admit embracing eliminative materialism, they are still shamelessly flirting with it.

Unlike Quine and Rorty, the two most prominent contemporary proponents of eliminative materialism, P. and P. Churchland, take with full seriousness the distinction between reductive and eliminative materialism. P.M. Churchland says,

> Eliminative materialism is the thesis that our commonsense conception of psychological phenomena constitutes a radically false theory, a theory so fundamentally defective that both the principles and the ontology of that theory will eventually be displaced, rather than smoothly reduced, by completed neuroscience.[9]

This is in clear contrast with reductive materialism:

> The identity theorist optimistically expects that folk psychology will be smoothly *reduced* by completed neuroscience, and its ontology preserved by dint of transtheoretic identities.

---

9 Paul M. Churchland, 'Eliminative Materialism and the Propositional Attitudes,' *The Journal of Philosophy*, **78** (1981): 67-90, 67.

Cast in this shape, what is at issue is the truth or falsity of competing theories. However, the Churchlands agree with Quine and Rorty inasmuch as they envision science playing an essential role: the true theory will be the one accepted by a 'completed neuroscience.' Fortunately, unlike Quine and Rorty, they are very clear that the issue of the future course of science really comes down to an issue much closer to home, namely the present truth about the mental. They eagerly pursue the course implied by this, namely a joint study of the best present theory/ies of the mental and the best present theory/ies of neuroscience.

It is shocking that neither P. nor P. Churchland actually *is* an eliminative materialist. When, in paper after paper, one or the other or both present the thesis and numerous arguments for it, as well as arguments against functionalism, Dennetism, epiphenomenalism, property dualism, etc., it is a letdown to find that they don't simply accept the conclusion for which they argue. For example, in *Neuroscience*, P.S. Churchland first dubs the present theory of the mental 'folk psychology,' and then goes on to call it an 'aboriginal conceptual network,' 'a stagnant research program,' one which 'will eventually find its place beside vitalism, animism, geocentrism and other curios of commensense science'[10]. Meanwhile, she roundly praises neuroscience. But she does not claim to be an eliminative materialist. In *The Journal of Philosophy* P.M. Churchland says that folk psychology 'is *at best* a highly superficial theory,' a 'stagnant or degenerating research program' one on a par with alchemy and vitalism[11]. Meanwhile he roundly praises neuroscience. But then he concludes merely that

> the principled displacement of folk psychology is not only richly possible, it represents one of the most intriguing theoretical displacements we can currently imagine.[12]

---

10 P.S. Churchland, 'Mind-Brain Reduction: New Light from the Philosophy of Science', *Neuroscience* 7 (1982) 1044-5

11 P.M. Churchland, 'Eliminative Materialism and the Propositional Attitudes,' 74-5

12 Ibid, 90

Rich possibility, that is a probability significantly higher than zero, can be claimed for most non-contradictory theses.

The question has to be asked: Why is there any logical exercise at all concerning eliminative materialism, since none of its proponents embrace it? The answer is plain: The mere possibility of eliminative materialism adds to the plausibility of materialism itself. Given the rule for the probability of disjoint disjunctions, if a new species of materialism is discovered and shown to be plausible, then the overall plausibility of materialism (i.e., that either reductive or eliminative materialism is correct) is equal to the sum of its prior plausibility plus the plausibility of the new species (since their joint plausibility is nil). So, strategically, eliminative materialism serves as a plausibility plumping device for materialism as a whole.

But it is when we turn from strategy to tactics that we find the most important use of eliminativism. In the present theatres of debate, it provides materialists with the armour to simply deflect certain sorts of attacks. When faced with a request to provide a positive account of how the human psyche, with its qualia, wants, pains, sense of humor, etc., is made of physical stuff, the materialist may run to the shelter of eliminativism, and simply deny that there are psyches, qualia, wants, pains, and so on. For example, the eliminativist is not troubled by the charge that he does not provide any materialistic accounts of belief or desire or wonder; all of these are so-called 'propositional attitudes,' thus part of folk psychology, and thus worthy of being simply ignored[13]. Another example is provided by P.S. Churchland when she advises a neuroscientific audience, whose members might understandably be worried about how their findings might somehow be made to cohere with either pedestrian or professional psychologies, simply to forget about this worry. Someday these psychologies will go the way of all folk psychology, she suggests, and a new, more powerful neuroscientific view of ourselves 'can become widely internalized'[14]. Yet another example is provided in 'Functionalism, Qualia, and Inten-

---

13 Ibid.; see especially 83-4.

14 P.S. Churchland, 'Mind-Brain Reduction,' see especially 1044-1045; quotation 1046

tionality,' where qualia and intentionality (as ordinarily understood) are denigrated, rather than explicated, in a dazzling display of eliminativist tactics. Consider just qualia, for example. It is conceded by the Churchlands that qualia exist (a surprise concession from eliminativists, but wait); in fact they are

> those intrinsic or monadic properties of our sensations discriminated in introspection.[15]

Proceeding materialistically, it is suggested that the

> intrinsic property might be the spiking frequency of the signal in some neural pathway, the voltage across a polarized membrane, the temporary deficit of some neurochemical, or the binary configuration of a set of DC pulses.

Our authors correctly anticipate the objection,

> "But *these* are not qualia!"[16]

To which they reply

> And why should such a property, or any of the others listed, *not* be the objective focus of introspective discrimination? To be sure, they would be *opaquely* discriminated, at least by creatures with a primitive self-conception like our own. That is to say, the spiking frequency of the impulses in a certain neural pathway need not prompt the non-inferential belief, "My pain has a spiking frequency of 60 Hz"; it may prompt only the belief, "My pain has a searing quality." But withal, the property you opaquely distinguish as "searingness" may be pricisely the property of having 60 Hz as a spiking frequency.[17]

---

15 Paul M. Churchland, and Patricia Smith Churchland, 'Functionalism, Qualia, and Intentionality,' *Philosophical Topics* **12** (1981), 121-45

16 Ibid., 128

17 Ibid.

Being a materialist, my reply is that there is no reason why searingness cannot be identified with some aspect of neural processes. Being candid, however, I must admit that this sort of (putative) identification still leaves a real and substantial puzzle: *how* is searingness to be constituted by the appropriate aspects of the appropriate processes? In other words, how is searingness to be *reduced* to the (presumably systemic) qualities of a physical process? Not recognizing any calls for reduction, the eliminativists will simply ignore my question. But it simply will not do to just say that searingness is a part of 'a primitive self conception,' and then to just ignore what searingness *seems* to us to be. Seemings, too, must be explained materialistically if materialism is to work. We need some account of why a spiking frequency of 60 Hz might seem searing (under whatever specific circumstances). *Not* that I would fault the Churchlands or any materialist for not having such an account in hand. But it seems to me to be a fault to not even recognize the need or desirability of such an account. The chemist may beg off giving an explanation of why saccharin seems sweet, by making dark references to the psychology of our olfactory perception: our brains 'interpret' saccharin (stimulation) as sugar (stimulation) – or whatever. But it is precisely *this* darkness which must be dispelled if materialism is to succeed. Materialists must anticipate the reduction of seeming sweetness and apparent searingness to physics. 'Interpretations' presumed to be performed by the brain are the work of homunculi, and must be renounced, as all good materialists know. But appearances of searingness, which it is averred are best ignored in favor of the corresponding reality of a 60 Hz spiking frequency, are no less the work of homunculi – until and unless the appearances too are *reduced*.

That seemings must be reduced to physics does not imply that everything we *say* about our seemings is true, and therefore must be accomodated by an adequate reduction. Our words and theories may systematically misrepresent our qualia, just as the Churchlands argue. A reduction of our qualia-as-experienced will require a more penetrating analysis of these qualia. At the present time, there is a tendency to treat qualia as unanalyzable, seamless wholes, completely given in the experiencing of them. No doubt experiences are, in a sense, given in the experience itself. But nothing is thereby given in the sense of 'datum,' where a datum is a report of some evidence, embedded in some theory, and thus correct, mistaken, perspicuous, misleading, etc. Bats experience qualia, but these experiences themselves are not data in the bats' theory of their own consciousness. Bats are too dumb for such things, and in any case, a qualium cannot itself be a datum *about* itself. Nor are qualia seamless and unanalyzable. The apparently seamless bouquet of a Cabernet Sauvignon may well be analyzed into its constituents by the connoisseur – and this holds for the bouquet-as-qualia as well as for the bouquet-as-vapor. The seemingly seamless major ninth chord may be resolved into its constituent notes by the musically trained, and so on and so on. Despite their eliminativism, the Churchlands themselves do much by way of analysis of qualia in several of their works[18], thus preparing the way for the reduction of said qualia. But like true eliminativists, they pursue the straight road of reduction only when it suits their purpose, and tarry at the wayside of eliminativism whenever the going gets rough[19].

So, in brief, eliminative materialism is propounded both as a way of inflating the plausibility of materialism and as a way of deflecting annoying challenges. My worry is that in covering the materialist's bald spots with eliminative camouflage, eliminativists may lull materialists into a false sense of security. So I shall hold eliminative materi-

---

18 Consider for example what they say about pain on pp. 125-6 of 'Functionalism, Qualia, and Intentionality', or what P.S. Churchland says in her 'Consciousness: The Transmutation of a Concept,' *Pacific Philosophical Quarterly* 64 (1983) 80-95.

19 It should also be pointed out that P.S. Churchland does not recommend the wholesale abandonment of folk psychology.

> There is no question of shelving folk psychology until there is a better theory to replace it with ... neuroscience needs to make use of prevailing folk psychological concepts in order to climb its way to a position where it can kick the ladder out from under. Pure bottom-up physiology would surely be pure exasperating folly.

Not that she is saying that there is any truth or insight contained in folk psychology – it has only a pragmatic, heuristic role to play ('Mind-Brain Reduction,' 1045-6).

alism up to criticism for the sake of anyone who is considering using it to defend materialism against the unrelenting attacks of the benighted anti-materialists. In such contests, where philosophy is at stake, it is best to know what is not reliable.

II. Problems with Eliminative Materialism

It is fair to say that the essence of eliminative materialism is the denial that there are such things, whether mental (heaven forbid!) *or* physical, as minds, imaginings, perceivings, raw-feels, inclinations, convictions, etc. If this is correct, then all of the bald spots of my materialism sprout hair. That there are no such things (let us call them m-things, m-processes, m-whatevers) is premised upon either or both of the following claims (though clearly these are not the only premises):

E+) M-language WILL be eliminated in favor of the idiom of neurophysiology.

E-) M-language is eliminABLE in favor of the idiom of neurophysiology.

Let's consider first E+, the claim that m-language *will* be eliminated in favor of the idiom of neurophysiology. The elimination of this language is, of course, intended to show the falsity of what is said in the language. One line of support for the claim is inspired by recent developments in the philosophy of science[20], and involves pointing out that

FP) M-language, which is putatively about m-processes, m-entities, m-properties, & c., and human behavior, is a theory.

---

20 P.S. Churchland is quite explicit about drawing lessons from the philosophy of science in her 'Mind-Brain Reduction: New Light from the Philosophy of Science,' 1041-4. P.K. Feyerabend is also quite explicit about it in his 'Mental Events and the Brain,' *Journal of Philosophy* 60 (1963) 295-6.

Let's benignly call it folk psychology, as eliminativists do. And

TR) Theories are replaced as better ones come along.

FP and TR have the advantage of being true – though TR is partial, showing only the optimistic half of the truth that theories are routinely replaced as better *or* worse ones come along. Philosophers, like everyone else, get the feeling that science is progressing over time, and various of them (e.g., Peirce, Popper, Carnap, Hempel, Lakatos, Laudan, ...) have tried to show that science progresses because of its peculiar methods and logic. Some conclude after sufficient argument that the logic of science guarantees (provided it is followed) that theories are replaced only by better ones. Yet Aristarchus' heliocentric truth was rejected by his geocentric colleagues, and Democritus' atomic truth replaced by false theories of matter. But I do not want to argue against scientific progress, and am happy enough with TR. Even so, TR and FP are not enough to establish E+, the prophecy that folk psychology will be replaced in favor of neurophysiology, for in themselves they do not imply which theory is better or replaceable. And so we find eliminative materialists making some supporting predictions:

NG) Neurphysiology will be a GOOD theory (in the relevant sense of 'good').

FB) Folk psychology will still be a BAD theory (in the relevant sense of 'bad').

As for FB, I am only too eager to agree with the eliminative materialist that folk psychology at least has some problems right now. No one can express the problems better than a promoter of eliminativism:

> When one centers one's attention not on what FP [folk psychology] can explain, but on what it cannot explain or fails even to address, one discovers that there is a very great deal. As examples of central and important mental phenomena that remain largely or wholly mysterious within the framework of FP, consider the nature and dynamics of mental illness, the faculty of

> creative imagination, or the ground of intelligence differences between individuals. Consider our utter ignorance of the nature and psychological functions of sleep, that curious state in which a third of one's life is spent. Reflect on the common ability to catch an outfield fly ball on the run, or hit a moving car with a snowball. Consider the internal construction of a 3-D visual image from subtle differences in the 2-D array of stimulations in our respective retinas. Consider the rich variety of perceptual illusions, visual and otherwise. Or consider the miracle of memory, with its lightening capacity for relevant retrieval. On these and many other mental phenomena, FP sheds negligible light.[21]

These areas do indeed represent failures of folk psychology. We should note, however, that with respect to mental illness, imagination, intelligence differences, sleep, catching outfield flies, 3-D imaging, illusions and memory, that *neuroscience has precious little to tell us either*. More importantly, as far as the issue at hand is concerned, we should not view these phenomena as territories contested by rival theories. Neuroscience could, after all, explain sleep or illusions without denying that there are such things as sleep or illusions. Neuroscience and folk psychology could co-exist peacefully.

Some attacks on folk psychology are more narrowly focussed against its use of propositional attitudes. As P.S. Churchland puts it,

> the heart of folk psychology is the belief-desire axis and now it must be emphasized that the signal fact about beliefs and desires is that they are *sentential attitudes*. What this means is that beliefs are always beliefs *that p*, where *p* is some sentence or other.[22]

Two objections are mounted against folk psychology because of this. Since,

> it implies that the brain's cognitive operations really are operations on sentences,
>
> First, it causes no end of trouble in dealing with the cognitive operations

---

21 Paul M. Churchland, 'Eliminative Materialism and the Propositional Attitudes,' 73.

22 P.S. Churchland, 'Mind-Brain Reduction,' 1045

> and intelligent behaviour of non-verbal humans; that is, preverbal children, deaf mutes, aphasics, etc. Second, it implies a radical discontinuity in the cognitive activity and information processing between verbal humans on the one hand and the rest of the animal kingdom on the other. Evolutionary considerations, on the contrary, would suggest that there are bound to be similarities.[23]

In reply to this it should be noted first of all that it does not follow from a folk psychologist's use of propositional attitudes that he thinks or implies that 'the brain's cognitive operations really are operations on sentences' – any more than the neurophysiologist's use of phrases such as 'There is a membrane potential of 2.3 volts' implies that he expects to find such *entities* as numbers or volts in the brain. Now *some* psychologists, notably Jerry Fodor, and many so-called 'cognitive scientists,' do indeed talk as though they expect to find sentences in the brain in some pretty unqualified sense – but not all folk psychologists need be persuaded of this[24]. The use of sentences *p, q, r,* in ascriptions of the form 'belief that *p*,' 'desire that *q*,' 'ignorance of *r*,' and so on, may be seen simply as an ascription of a representation state to a person – however such states may be instantiated by grey matter. An algorithm may be provided to show how a more perspicuous paraphrase may be accomplished: 'X believes that *p*' means 'X's neural states (and/or processes) include a representation state p* which contains the same information (roughly) as the sentence *p* and which X takes to be accurate.' In the case of desires, the phrase 'takes to be accurate' is replaced by 'takes to be desirable'; in the case of ignorance of *p*, understand this either to indicate the absence of the representation state itself, or replace 'takes to be accurate' by 'takes to be inaccurate.' And so on[25]. Secondly, it simply does not follow that the proposi-

---

23 Ibid.

24 I am in agreement with the criticisms of mentalese marshalled by Patricia Smith Churchland, 'Language, Thought, and Information Processing,' *Nous* 14 (1980) 147-70. For a presentation of a pro-mentalese theory, see Jerry Fodor, *The Language of Thought* (New York: Crowell 1975).

25 The 'takes to be in/accurate' and 'wants to be accurate' in the above formulation leave intact the 'attitude' involved in any 'propositional attitude' while

tional attitude conceptual machinery cannot apply to prelinguistic or non-linguistic minds or brains. Animals and pre-verbal children *do* see, hear, perceive, remember, want, avoid, try, and so on. What is wrong with expressing what it is they want, avoid, and so on, by means of language – why not, in fact, use sentences? We may know, for example, that the little girl won't go into the yard because she sees the dog, and is afraid of dogs – though she is preverbal and has never spoken or thought a word in her life. How can we otherwise express what is going on here, and in any case why should we try to find some other means of expression? As long as we do not picture sentences in her head, there is no harm in saying that she sees that *there is a dog in the yard*. There is no harm in saying the same sort of thing about the non-linguistic dog: the dog likes children, likes to lick their faces – but we do not dream that there is a word 'children' in the dog's brain, nor do we imply any such thing. P.M. Churchland fleshes out the same problem:

> One particularly outstanding mystery is the nature of the learning process itself, especially wher it involves large-scale conceptual change, and especially as it appears in its pre-linguistic or entirely nonlinguistic form (as in infants and animals), which is by far the most common form in nature. FP is faced with special difficulties here, since its conception of learning as the manipulation and storage of propositional attitudes founders on the fact that how to formulate, manipulate, and store a rich fabric of propositional attitudes is itself something that is learned, and is only one among many acquired cognitive skills. FP would thus appear constitutionally incapable of even addressing this most basic of mysteries.[26]

---

dispensing with the 'proposition.' Having an 'attitude' towards a representation state is not, I think, one bit less intuitive than having an attitude towards a proposition or sentence. However, I realize that the 'attitude' itself is a neural process or state. These 'attitudes' may be given a dispositional characterization at this time along the following lines: a representation state is believed iff it is acted upon in the appropriate circumstances; a representation state is accurate if its possessor acts to make the world correspond to his representation under the appropriate circumstances, etc. A very long digression would be required to flesh out these schemas; instead, see my 'A Rule Of Minimal Rationality,' cited below, or P.M. Churchland's 'The Logical Character of Action Explanations', *Philosophical Review* 79 (1970) 214-36.

26 Paul M. Churchland, 'Eliminative Materialism and the Propositional Attitudes,' 73-4

Despite its ring of plausibility, the charge is mislaid. It is unjustifiable to aver that folk psychology is limited to the machinery of propositional attitudes simply because it sometimes uses this machinery: we do not, after all, limit neurophysiology to chemistry, even though it sometimes appeals to chemistry. Secondly, as I have been arguing above, *even if* folk psychology were limited to the propositional attitude as its idiom, this does not render it 'constitutionally incapable of even addressing' the psychology of pre- or non-verbal animals (such as children). For example, there is a folk psychological theory of language-learning which clearly contains some real information. I shall recall only some of the most obvious pieces of this theory in order to make the point: the child remembers some of what she sees and hears, as do animals of some other species. This explains why she won't learn the word 'psychology' unless she sees it or hears it. It explains why she will not learn the word 'dog' unless she can see some dog or dog picture, or hear or read a dog description. It explains why Chinese children typically learn Chinese, while students of physics learn words like 'mass' and 'acceleration.' It correctly instructs us to check the hearing of children who don't learn to speak, and the vision of those who can't learn to read. It correctly leads us to suspect a range of other disadvantages among those who cannot acquire linguistic skills despite having adequate vision and hearing, disadvantages ranging from general learning disability to dyslexia. If it seems that folk psychology isn't offering much here, this must be balanced against the fact that neuroscience offers much less.

Eliminative materialists delight in pointing out the failure of folk psychological kinds like hearing and remembering to match newfangled neurophysiological kinds like neuron and hypothalamus[27].

---

27 As P.M. Churchland puts it,

> FP's explanatory impotence and long stagnation inspire little faith that its categories will find themselves neatly reflected in the framework of neuroscience

on p. 75 of his 'Eliminative Materialism and the Propositional Attitudes.' There is no doubt that this is seen as a serious charge. However, see below.

But the mismatch may be no more telling than the failure of chronometric kinds like escapement mechanism to match physical kinds like iron – yet no one hesitates to reduce a clock to physics, much less to deny the existence of escapement mechanisms. No one believes that there is any need to appeal to anything non-physical to explain the actual (as opposed to the ideal) behavior of the clock. The changes of angular momenta of the bodies called 'gears,' the flexing of the body called the 'hairspring,' the chemical reactions between oil and metal, all may be explained by physics. Nothing would be gained by appeal to emergent properties, the function of the clock or its parts, or a chronometric ghost in the machine. Nor need the behavior that we explain be expressed in the idiom of physics. 'Gear' and 'hairspring' are not categories of physics. We can explain, solely by appeal to physics, why the clock runs slow or why it breaks down at a certain time, though 'runs slow' and 'breaks down' are not part of the conceptual machinery of physics. In the case of this transparent reduction of a mechanism to physics, at least two things are apparent:

1. There is no necessity for the concepts of the reduced theory to map neatly onto the concepts of the reducing theory. There is no need for a definition function from one theory to the other, or for 'bridge laws' between them. A purely contingent identification of something in the reduced domain with something in the reducing domain is sufficient: e.g., this gear is a body having physical dimensions *d*, *d'*, *d''*,...

2. Even where two theories having non-intertranslatable conceptual schemes, schemes not inter-related by bridge-laws, share some domain, it does not follow that at least one of the theories must be rejected. Both theories may be acceptable. Neither need be eliminated. For example, there is no need to deny the existence of escapement mechanisms simply because they do not appear in the ontology of physics alongside electron and positron.

We shall have occasion to return to these two points later on.

Meanwhile, despite all of its admitted shortcomings, folk

psychology sustains us on a day to day basis[28]. We successfully predict the future and reconstruct the past using it and it alone. If we possess no other information about an individual than the folk psychological description of her as very shy, then we know that she will not flirt with the waiter or dance on the table in a restaurant. Our form of life depends vitally and successfully on such folk psychology. The degree of certainty we can obtain with such methods can be very high. In some cases, a precision may be achieved which rivals that achievable in physics. For example, we may make plans to meet at a certain spot at a certain date months or years in advance, and succeed in doing so with extremely small spatial or temporal error. I may then predict your presence at the spot solely on the basis of folk psychological information years in advance, and with an error of only a few feet and a few seconds. It would be extremely difficult to achieve the same degree of accuracy in the prediction of the position of the earth itself years from now. And the domain of such informations is not restricted to the deliberate activities of linguistically adept adults. Prelinguistic children may also be shy, may nevertheless remember seeing us before, recognize us, etc., etc. Since neurophysiology is pretty much a nonstarter in cases like these – perhaps 'constitutionally incapable of even addressing' such phenomena – we would be well advised to put off the elimination of folk psychology until a more propitious time. Since talk about m-things is a thorn in my materialistic side, perhaps I should be happy to see m-things impugned. Certainly I would not mind seeing folk psychology budged out of the position of sacred mystery that it now seems to hold in the brains of so many. However, it is plainly unwarranted in the absence of a replacement for folk psychology to premise E+, its actual (future) elimination, on FB, a complaint about its power.

This brings us to considering neurophysiology, the proposed and promoted replacement for folk psychology. How do eliminative materialists argue in favor of NG, the claim that neurophysiology will be a good theory? The argument usually consists in compiling

---

28 I have outlined the virtues of folk psychology in 'A Rule of Minimal Rationality: The Logical Link between Beliefs and Values.' *Inquiry* 19 (1976) 341-53.

references to the successes of neurophysiology, the more recondite the better. This silences the critics, as it is difficult to object to sophisticated scientific findings. Not that any materialist should have anything against neuroscience, since it supports materialism (more on this below). Nevertheless, the use of it as an argument in favor of *eliminative* materialism is not quite scrutable. Since eliminative materialists deny the existence of m-entities, m-processes, etc., they abjure the sort of neurophysiological researches which study interconnections between processes in the nervous system and conscious experiences. According to strict advocates, there are no conscious experiences. So when asked to support their rosy prognosis for neuroscience, NG, they refer to neurophysiological successes in explaining the eye movements of monkeys or some of the behavior of sea slugs[29] (*aplysia*). You don't have to worry so much about anyone championing raw-feels in sea slugs or monkeys (although, see Nagel.[30]) But, somehow, the very recondite unravelling of the nervous systems of monkeys and slugs is not as convincing a datum in favor of materialism as some not very recondite neurophysiological facts, such as that tampering with one's eyes can cause visual sensation, or that tampering with one's brain can put one's lights out completely. The crude neurophysiological fact that tampering with certain parts of my nervous system causes certain alterations in my consciousness places consciousness and nervous system in the same causal network, at least, even if it does not go so far as to establish identities between processes of the two sorts. But note that the complexity of the brain with its 100,000,000,000 neurons, each with possibly thousands of connections to others, and to sensory mechanisms, is strong evidence in favour of materialism. If the head contained a lump of bone marrow called the 'brain,' then we would have had to conclude, along with Aristotle, that it is not the seat of the soul. This would have been a

---

29 See, e.g., P.S. Churchland's 'A Perspective on Mind-Brain Research,' *The Journal Of Philosophy* 77 (1980) 198-206; or 'Brain States,' by Kathleen V. Wilkes, *British Journal For The Philosophy Of Science* **31** (1980) 111-29.

30 Thomas Nagel, 'What It Is Like To Be A Bat,' *Philosophical Review* 83 (1974) 443-50.

death-blow to materialism: nothing else in the body has the sort of active complexity and sensitivity to qualify as our conscious self. Since the brain supplies potential falsification of materialism, it supplies potential verification too. Given what the brain actually is, it is actual confirmation of materialism (though not conclusive verification).

I have nothing against neuroscience. It is fine stuff. I'm not as sanguine about its future as the eliminative materialist, but – and this is the essential point – I don't see why one needs to be. Sufficient neurophysiological study has already been done to show the high plausibility of materialism. A materialist need not mortgage his philosophy to the future success of neuroscience. Given that we have come to expect any science to rewrite itself periodically, and to expect that neuroscience is no exception to the rule, a too rosy optimism is inconsistent with philosophic (or scientific) realism. With suitable caveats, I'm pretty optimistic too, in my realistic way: allowing for theoretical revolutions in relevant fields, providing human beings don't suffer a nuclear holocaust or Velikovskyan cataclysm, and so on, science will unravel our brains, and thereby explicate our consciousness. If this is achieved, then we will understand why we see, hear, smell, taste, and imagine the things we do, whether standing with our eyes open in broad daylight, or dreaming in our beds. However, I believe this *because* I'm a materialist, rather than conversely, as in the case of the eliminative materialist. I expect that all of the sundry facts about people and their minds, from the effect of aspirin on headaches to the effect of marrying upon loneliness, will be explained in the fullness of time by science, *because* sundry facts of this sort convince me that people are physical, or, what amounts to the same thing, susceptible to being explained scientifically, i.e., by reference to their physical conditions. Neuroscience has yet to explain headaches or their removal by aspirin, explain loneliness or love, let alone my occasional embarassment at being a materialist. But we can now explain quite a few things neurophysiologically. For instance, after-images may be explained in terms of the habituation (or fatigue) of the nervous tissues involved in vision. It is fair to say that the visual experience I get with my glasses removed has been scientifically explained – that is, that myopia has been reduced to physics. However, these newer sorts of explanation are of the same sort as the ones available for millenia: causal connections between one's experience and the state of one's eyes, ears, nerves, brain, and other parts. However, it will not accrue much to the favor of materialism to explain the *behavior* of monkeys, sea slugs, even of ourselves, in neurophysiological terms. Our headaches, loves, dreams, afterimages, thoughts, even our philosophies – in short, our conscious doings – have to be explained in neurophysiological terms if neurophysiology is to speak loudly in favor of materialism. This, I submit, it does and continues to do with ever more clarity.

At this time, despite failings on both sides, reductive materialism and neuroscience are not adversaries, but allies. If there are reasons to doubt NG, that neurophysiology will be a good theory, they come from scientific considerations, not metaphysical ones. In the present spurt of growth in the science the ratio of questions discovered to questions answered seems much greater than one. The complexity is truly boggling, and no more than the vaguest sketches are now available of whole-system functioning[31]. There is also the disquieting possibility that the nervous system may at points be sensitive to micro-events on the quantum level. The eye can see a single photon, and there is no reason yet to rule out similar degrees of sensitivity at other points in the nervous system. Naturally occurring radioactive isotopes in the body could no doubt cause neurons to fire. This suggests the possibility that neuroscience could be infected with the barriers to complete knowledge that we now believe obtain at the microlevel. The marriage of complexity and incompleteness has darkness as

---

31 The most noteworthy account of whole-system functioning is the metric tensor network theory proposed by A. Pellionisz and R. Llinas. For an outline of their theory and a bibiliography, see 'Space-Time Representation In The Brain. The Cerebellum As A Predictive Space-Time Metric Tensor,' *Neuroscience* 7 (1982) 2949-70. See also Andras J. Pellionisz, 'Brain Theory: Connecting Neurobiology to Robotics. Tensor Analysis: Natural Coordinates to Describe, Understand, and Engineer Functional Geometries of Intelligent Organisms' *Journal of Theoretical Neurobiology* 2 (1983), no. 3. It is interesting to note that in this theory, a very strong and clear meaning is given to the notion that there are representations in the nervous system of the external (or even of the internal) world. Roughly speaking, the representation is the invariant maintained through a series of tranformations of a neural state-vector by a series of metric tensors; see especially the first work listed above.

its offspring. The insolubility of the three-body problem in Newtonian mechanics (incompleteness) presently makes it difficult to know even how many moons there are in the Saturnian system (complexity), because we cannot compute their interacting orbits with enough accuracy to keep track of individual satellites. We can expect to solve the Saturnian system with its dozen or so satellites in due time, but the nervous system with its 100,000,000,000,000 neurons, each with as many as thousands of dendritic connections to others, any of which may at any time be behaving in a indeterministic manner, is not a system which will be solved soon. We may have to settle for roadmaps of the major connections, and very fragmentary knowledge of the traffic thereon. So it goes.

But even if we forget these worries, and hypothesize that neuroscience will be completely successful in laying bare the mysteries of the brain, there is no evidence that it will *eliminate* folk psychology. So, compounded upon the speculative business of scrying the development of neuroscience is the speculative business of seeing just what form the prophesied success will take. The quantum mechanical explanation of everyday objects like tables and chairs is in the relevant sense completely successful, and in the relevant sense better than the folk theory of everyday objects. Nevertheless, it simply is untrue that it has eliminated the very unsophisticated, primitive, stagnant, error-ridden folk theory. With reference to both E+ and E- , we must realize that it is untrue that we could get by referring to tables, chairs, Alberta crude, and the ace of spades by their quantum mechanical descriptions. Nor is it plausible to say that there are no such things as tables, chairs, Alberta crude, or the ace of spades. This shows that there is an onus upon the eliminative materialist to convince us also of

EF) The becoming good of neurophysiology, NG, and the remaining bad of folk psychology, FB, will obtain in such a way as to result in the elimination of folk psychology.

But producing conviction about EF is made difficult by the fact that there has been no general agreement among philosophers concerning what makes some changes in scientific doctrine more like the now fashionable model of the overthrow and liquidation of the old theory by the new (e.g., the elimination of Aristotelian mechanics by

Newtonian mechanics, the elimination of phlogistic theory by the theory of oxidation), and what makes others take on the character of good old fashioned theory reduction (e.g., the reduction of Newtonian mechanics to a limiting case of either quantum of relativistic mechanics). As we have seen earlier, the sort of incommensurability that amounts to the lack of interdefinition or the lack of bridge-laws is no bar to explanatory reduction of one theory to another: chronometric phenomena can be reduced to physics, though chronometry contains teleological categories (such as escapement mechanism, bearing, gear, etc.) which are indefinable in pure physics. Ontologically, we can and do believe that there exist both escapement mechanisms and molecules, just as we believe that there are both playing cards and their micro-structures.

It is *difficult* to see just what it is in general that makes theories eliminable. This is not surprising, for it amounts to the fact that we cannot see in general just what it is that makes theories false. It would clearly be the greatest boon ever to fall to our intellectual history to have such a test for falsity. We don't have it. However, in general, disputes between theories may lead to a range of results, from survival of the fittest alone to peaceful coexistence of all parties. Now, the eliminative materialist is claiming that in addition to granting the envisaged relationship between neuroscience and folk psychology outlined in NG and FB, we must grant that there will be conflict between the theories, and that it will result in the elimination of one party, namely folk psychology. But this scenario is the instantiation of the leftmost of a whole spectrum of possibilities. The eliminative materialist *must* claim this because to whatever degree the outcome approximates theory reduction rather than elimination, the identity theory, rather than the eliminative theory, is (to that degree) correct. But, just as folk properties of paint, say, such as that it dries on the walls to which it adheres, may be explained *rather than eliminated* by reference to its chemistry and the chemistry of the atmosphere and wall, so too may the folk psychological properties of people be explained rather than eliminated by neuroscience. No one thinks that neurophysiology, no matter how advanced, will eliminate the wine connoisseur's appreciation of wine. What, then, makes the eliminativist bank on the idea that we will cease to take literally the idea that wine connoisseurs like wine because of its taste and aroma rather than out of thirst? Of course, it is not enough for the eliminativist to say merely that we will be able to express in a more faithful idiom the relationship between wines and tasters now captured in saying that the latter appreciate the former because of its taste rather than their thirst, since this would amount to functionalism or the identity theory. He categorically denies the existence of tastes, aromas, thirsts, etc., since each is folk psychological to the core. But surely folk psychology is not *so* far from the truth that it is wrong that the sensations (which materialists realize are neural processes) produced by the interaction of wine and tongue are the sine qua non of the wine connoisseur's world. Clearly the eliminative materialist owes us sufficient argument to show that all such accounts are false.

In fact, it is hard to come up with historical cases of genuine theory elimination. *Parts* of a theory may go down. The geocentric spheres of Aristotle were eliminated by Hipparchus and Ptolemy – but that is not to say that Aristotelians knew nothing about the stars and planets. They observed the same Sun, Moon, and planets we see today. They did not look for them in their beds, and the doctors who subscribed to the demon theory of disease did not look for patients in the sky. So even Aristotelian astronomy and the demon theory of disease were not completely eliminated by newer, truer sciences. Yet Aristotelian astronomy and the demon theory of disease are paradigms of eliminated theory. Surely it is a safe bet that folk psychology is not utterly eliminable either. But eliminativists do not identify a part of folk psychology which is to be eliminated – they say the whole is to be considered false. Eliminative materialism is on a par with claiming the sun, moon, planets, and diseases themselves just as unreal as the spheres and demons. Eliminativists do not say, e.g., chagrin will or might prove unreal while headache will or might not. Yet some folk psychological items seem poor candidates for elimination. Sleep is a folk psychological concept – is there no such thing as sleep? The concept shows every sign of being assimilated by neuroscience. The scientific journal, *Sleep*, is largely comprised of neuroscientific works, as is the journal *Pain*. To prophesy the the elimination of folk psychology without qualification is to ignore the history of previous scientific revolutions, and to ignore present neuroscience as well.

So foretelling the type of the prophesied neuroscience revolution is a slippery business, but one sadly essential to eliminative materialism.

When we do manage to get some traction on the issue, moreover, there is much evidence for doubting the hoped-for revolution will take the hoped-for shape of theory elimination rather than theory reduction[32].

What about a weaker eliminative materialism premised on E-, the claim that m-language is eliminABLE in favor of the idiom of neurophysiology? Here there is a range of cases corresponding to a range of senses for the word 'eliminable.' In the strongest sense of the word, E- amounts to the claim that m-language is eliminable by neurophysiology in a pragmatic, daily idiom sense. But this claim, as we have seen, is dicey. In the weakest sense of the word, E- amounts to the claim that m-language is eliminable in principle, in the sense that all theories with empirical content (or without, perhaps) are eliminable in principle – that is, may turn out to be radically false or misconceived. But this claim is much too weak to do service for materialism, for in the fullness of time neurophysiology may pass away just as may folk psychology. So eliminative materialism has to define some sense of 'eliminable' between the two extremes. Presumably the most promising sense of eliminability is eliminability in theory, the sense in which 'the queen of spades' is eliminable, in the lab but not in a poker game, by its quantum mechanical description. Indeed, I expect it is just this sort of eliminability eliminativists using E- would favor. As P.S. Churchland says,

---

32 Some eliminative materialists (Michael Stack, in conversation, and Paul Churchland, both in conversation and in correspondence) try to shift the burden of proof to the reductive materialists in this way: they say, 'We both agree that materialism (let's call it thesis M) is true. You believe that folk psychology, F, is true, at least in part. Your reductive materialism, therefore, commits you to M & F, whereas my eliminative materialism commits me merely to M. So the a priori probability is in my favor, since a priori the probability of p is greater that the probability of p & q in general. Therefore, the onus is upon you to defend your commitment to F, in addition to your commitment to M. So, my commitments are less extensive than your own.' The proper reply to this is that the eliminative materialist is really committed to M & $\neg$F, which has the same a priori probability as M & F. Therefore the onus is no more upon the reductivist to defend folk psychology than it is upon the eliminativist to attack it.

> in the first instance the replacement is a theoretical reduction in the sense specified earlier [which, by her sense of "reduction," includes replacement as a species; cf. 1043] ... Whether the reducing theory becomes common coin depends on many non-theoretical factors.[33]

Presumably the 'non-theoretical factors' here include that we cannot see the enormous complexes of micro-detail which comprise nervous processes — though we might infer their presence on the basis of folk observation.

However, E- in this sense is nevertheless beleaguered and wounded. For one thing, if neurophysiology could replace folk psychology in theory, then the converse could happen as well. In fact, even dualists and idealists could appeal to eliminability in theory. Berkeley's program of eliminating the material idiom in favor of the ideal may be quite impossible in the sense of pragmatic elimination, as Quine, among others, has convincingly argued. But there is no obstacle to such an elimination in the laboratory of the idealist. That is, any statement in the garden-variety material object idiom may be replaced by its counterpart in the idiom of idealism. 'I see a chair' can be replaced by the right description of my sensations, at least in the laboratory, even if there are insurmountable problems concerning daily use of the idealist idiom, or the teaching of it to children as a first language, and so on. So, if E- is to be a major premise of eliminative materialism, some principle must be adduced which will tell us which of the possible eliminations in theory are to be disregarded and which is to be embraced as metaphysically relevant. The principle which the eliminativists seems to be invoking here is this: Where theory A is much better than theory B, and where B is eliminable in theory in favor of A, then the entities (processes, properties, laws, etc.) of B should be thought unreal (false, etc.) and those of A thought real.

But, if the arguments I have presented are sound, there are several objections to this procedure, each sufficient to block the way of the eliminative materialist. The first is that it is unwarranted right now to declare m-things unreal on the grounds that there is *hope* that neurophysiology will prove to be a much better theory than folk

33 P.S. Churchland, 'Mind-Brain Reduction,' 1046

psychology. The most that can be maintained in good conscience is that there is hope that m-things will prove to be unreal. Secondly, as we have seen, the hope does not seem very well founded. There is much to be said for folk psychology, and much to be said against neurophysiology. There is nothing that we can as yet substitute for the present co-operation of the two theories. In fact, it seems quite obvious that we could at least get along without neurophysiology, but that we could not get along at present without folk psychology. Thirdly, the principle (mentioned in the last paragraph) involved in the use of E- is simply false. The unreality of the entities of a poorer theory does not follow from the acceptance of a better theory operating in the same domain. The better theory itself must be incompatible with the ontology of the poorer theory. We have seen an example (and there are many others) of ontological compatibility between the folk theory of physical objects and the far better quantum theory. That neuroscience and folk psychology are incompatible is sorely wanting evidence or demonstration. Indeed, there is evidence of their compatibility in the wholesale co-operation of the two.

III. Conclusion

So I conclude that the eliminative materialist has done little to ease my embarassment at being a materialist. What he has done, he has done unintentionally, by making me see just how much of current neuroscience provides evidence that materialism of a reductive form will win out in the end. I thank him for his help, but I note that Lucretius has done just as much, perhaps more, for he has shown me how to rest the case for materialism on less recondite, less controversial, more time-tested evidence. And Lucretius provides me with the inspiration to embarass my antagonists even as I am embarassed. For instance, he suggests

> It is hard to maintain that the eyes see nothing and that the mind looks through them as if through open doors ... if our eyes serve as doors, it seems that the mind ought to see things more clearly if the eyes were removed, yes the very door and doorposts as well.[34]

---

34 Lucretius, *On Nature*, translated by Russell M. Geer, Library of Liberal Arts, Bobbs-Merrill, 1965, 359-60.

At least we old fashioned materialists know why we don't want to eliminate our eyes *or* our minds.

Received April, 1983

CANADIAN JOURNAL OF PHILOSOPHY
Supplementary Volume 11

Sensation, Theory and Meaning[1]

B. THURSTON and S. COVAL
University of British Columbia
Vancouver, BC V6T 1W5

I

One way to judge whether sensations are merely part of the causal order and not part of the cognitive or epistemic order is to determine whether or not sensations control to any extent the meaning of our observation terms. Should our observation terms have their meanings

1 We would like to thank Michael Feld and Gary Wedeking for reading and commenting on the original draft of this paper. We are also indebted to Jack MacIntosh whose reply at the Western Canadian Philosophical Association Meetings, (Regina, 1980) was helpful as were the comments of Paul Churchland in a letter occasioned by his exposure to that same version. We are grateful as well for the comments of an anonymous referee for the *Canadian Journal of Philosophy*.

even in part determined by sensations then this would seem to be evidence that sensations are of the cognitive order. In a recent and noteworthy book, *Scientific Realism and the Plasticity of Mind,* Paul Churchland offers a development of the Sellarsian idea that sensations play a merely causal role in perception.[2] Churchland also cites Paul Feyerabend,[3] whose adaptation of the Sellarsian position he finds more to his purpose. The central argument of Churchland's book and the one which will be most particularly dealt with herein is an attempt to show that facts about sensations are totally irrelevant to the meaning of observation terms, even to the meaning of common observation terms such as 'hot,' 'cold,' 'white,' and 'black.' It is Churchland's contention, then, that facts about the intrinsic nature of sensations (as opposed to facts about their roles in causal chains) are semantically irrelevant. Even the causal role which sensations at present enjoy in determining the meaning of observation terms might, Churchland suggests, be dispensed with provided 'there remain systematic causal connections between [some, non-sensory] kinds of states of affairs and kinds of singular judgements.'[4]

The implications of such a semantic argument, if it could be persuasively made, would, Churchland claims, have a subclimax in the area of philosophy of mind and a climax in that of epistemology. Thus in the area of philosophy of mind its implications would be of vital importance, he thinks, to the eliminative materialist. To show that the meaning of common observation terms is without a sensory core would be to show that these terms and the 'common-sense' conceptual framework of which they are a part, are as thoroughly theoretical, and therefore *as potentially eliminable in the face of advancing knowledge,* as are the observation terms of any other theoretical framework, frameworks such as the molecular, the electro-magnetic, the Newtonian, or the Einsteinian. The '[Sellarsian] prospect we face,'

---

2 Paul M. Churchland, *Scientific Realism and the Plasticity of Mind,* Cambridge University Press (1979), 5

3 Ibid., 15; Paul Feyerabend, 'Science Without Experience,' *Journal of Philosophy,* 66, no. 22 (1969)

4 Churchland, *Scientific Realism and the Plasticity of Mind,* 15

says Churchland, 'is that a detailed neurophysiological conception of ourselves might simply displace our mentalistic self-conception.'[5]

Churchland claims additionally for his argument that it would, if successful, serve to make possible the climax which he seeks in epistemology by virtue of clearing away objections to his claim that we are 'epistemic engines.' An 'epistemic engine,' for Churchland, is that to which information about the intrinsic nature of sensations is properly seen to be of only 'narrow' and 'parochial' concern[6] and to which 'the construction of an internal "model" that can systematically mime sundry dimensions of the environment is ... the essence of ... intellectual development.'[7]

It is the purpose of the present paper to undermine these two claims: that what we are is in any way adequately captured by the phrase 'epistemic engines' and that 'a detailed neurophysiological conception of ourselves might simply displace our mentalistic self-conception.' It is our contention that, while the sub-conclusion for which Churchland strives is almost certainly right – viz., that our common-sense self-conception is not only a theory but a far from perfect theory at that – neither is it the case that this sub-conclusion presupposes that facts about the intrinsic natures of sensations are irrelevant to the meanings of our common observation terms, nor is it the case that the eliminative materialist conclusion which Churchland ultimately seeks follows from this sub-conclusion. Thus on the one hand, nothing nearly so strong as the irrelevance of facts about sensations is required to demonstrate the theoretical nature of our common-sense framework. And on the other hand, and contrary to what Churchland – and apparently Sellars and Feyerabend as well – assumes, to demonstrate that our common-sense framework is theoretical and hence possibly false is not, thereby, to lend any support to the claims of the eliminative materialist. That our present 'mentalistic' self-conception leads us to fail to exploit, or to mis-exploit, vast amounts of objective information retrievable from the

5 Ibid., 5

6 Ibid., 6

7 Ibid., 149

patterns discernable in our sensory experiences does not entail, or even in any way enhance the possibility of, the falsity of our present self-conception *as mentalistic*. Our present common-sense world view might well undergo radical revision while the mentalistic aspect of the self-conception intrinsic to that view remains unscathed. If that were so, it would surely be obvious that epistemic engines cannot be what we are. Epistemic engines are exceedingly complex measuring instruments, filtering and processing information automatically and for no reason at all (except because it's there). Human beings, as essentially mentalistic entities, do indeed filter and process information, albeit inefficiently; but always with an eye to what use it can be put in controlling the flow of *mental states*: of *sensations* and *feelings*.

As the cornerstone of Churchland's materialistic endeavour, then, his argument for the irrelevance of sensations to the meaning of common observation terms will be the main target of our attack.

II

We are asked to imagine that a set of aliens, (*A*s), exist whose members are in all respects similar to us, earthlings (*E*s), with the exception that they have visual sensations in respect of the objective parameter, temperature, where we *E*s have tactile ones. Where something feels hot, warm or cold to *E*s, *A*s correspondingly have visual images of white, grey or black. (*A*s do not possess any sensory information about the objective parameter which causes colour experiences in *E*s.) We are also asked to suppose that *A*s use the same words or sounds in making their visual reports of the objective parameter, temperature, as we do in making our tactile reports of that same parameter. Since this parameter affects them, at least under a definable set of 'normal' conditions, in ways which are systematically correlatable with the ways in which it affects us, we will make, each in our respective languages, belief utterances which will, in a superficial sense at least, be strictly identical. We will each utter, or be disposed to assent to the utterance of, such strings of words as: 'Fires are hot'; 'A warm thing will warm up a cooler thing but never the reverse'; and the like. The question is: Are our utterances identical *only* in the superficial sense that they consist of identical strings of sounds or are they also identical in the further and deeper sense that they have the same meaning?

Churchland, as has already been indicated, designed the above-described imaginary case with the intention of providing a means of testing theories about the meaning of common observation , terms such as 'hot.' In particular, he hopes to show that this test case provides conclusively damaging counter-evidence to a theory, taken from 'the crude intuitions supplied by common-sense,'[8] according to which the meaning of such terms 'is given in sensation.'[9] Thus, on the common-sense view, the truth or falsity of a statement about, say, the colour of an object, depends to some extent or other on facts about the intrinsic natures of sensations caused by sensory exposure to that object. The common-sense, or sensationalist theory, can take one of two forms, Churchland suggests, one of which is much stronger than the other. (Churchland, as we will see, concentrates his attack on the stronger thesis which, as should become obvious, is the decidedly less plausible of the two.) According to the strongest form of the sensationalist thesis, the meaning of common observation terms is given *wholly* in terms of facts about the intrinsic natures of sensations; on a weaker version, it is determined only *partly* by such facts.

The case involving *A*s and *E*s provides a test for the strongest version of this theory about the meaning of common observation terms in the following way: The correct theory about the meaning of this class of terms, whatever it might be, must allow for translations between the two languages, *A* and *E,* which preserve the truth values of the original observation utterances. We must, that is, as *E*s, be able to attribute largely true beliefs to *A*-utterers; be able to avoid any theory of meaning which would force us to translate in such a way as to '[make] a joke of their beliefs and visual capabilities.'[10] Churchland finds the claim that theories of meaning must meet such a condition to be particularly persuasive in light of the fact that the total reciprocity of the

8 Ibid., 8

9 Ibid., 10

10 Ibid., 10

situation would force the *A*s to attribute largely false beliefs to *us*, to make the same joke of our beliefs and visual capabilities, on any theory which forced us to attribute largely false beliefs to *them*. If, then, we are to be able to make any sense of each other's utterances, and not, that is, to each find the other's observation statements to be ridiculously and consistently out of keeping with our own, we must have a theory of meaning which generates only mutually truth preserving translations.

It is this condition that the more extreme view which Churchland attributes to common-sense apparently fails to fulfill. What Churchland takes to be a common-sense view of the meaning of common observation terms such as 'hot' would generate the ascription of false beliefs, by *A*s to *E*s and vice versa, in the following way. Remember that the *A*s have, as a causal consequence of exposure to that same objective parameter which is causally responsible for sensations of *heat* in *us*, visual sensations of *white*. (Except where otherwise indicated, all use of words such as 'hot' and 'white' will involve the *E*, that is our, system of meanings.) Further, their verbal behavior in such situations is strikingly similar to ours; they say, in *A*, of the object at which they are looking when they are having a sensation of the sort which we characteristically have in the visual presence of white objects, just what we say, in *E*, of the same object if we are touching it and having a sensation of heat; namely, 'It is hot.' Now according to the strongest form of the sensationalist theory of meaning we must, it seems, given the fact that the sensation characteristically associated, for them, with the claim that *x* is hot is that sensation which we call a sensation of white, translate utterances, by *A*s, of '*x* is hot' as '*x* is white.' But, except for occasional coincidences where an object is both (what we would call) hot *and* white, this translation procedure would have us ascribe to the *A*s false beliefs. Clearly, Churchland believes, such a sensationalist view about the meaning of observation terms will require the systematic attribution of false beliefs by us to any being who fails to share exactly our sensory modalities. In showing this, the device of invoking imaginary *A*s has, he believes, thereby provided a *reductio ad absurdum* of the common-sense position, or at least of the strongest version of that position. He proposes as an alternative to this unworkable wholly sensation-guided translation procedure a strictly non-sensationalist one according to which 'networks of beliefs [are] the bearers or determinants of understanding.'[11] The theoretical basis for Churchland's proposed non-sensationalist translation procedure is the contention that:

> ... the meaning of the relevant observation terms has nothing to do with the intrinsic qualitative identity of whatever sensations just happen to prompt their non-inferential application in singular empirical judgements. Rather, their position in semantic space appears to be determined by the network of sentences containing them accepted by speakers who use them.[12]

He considers, and cursorily dismisses, the possibility that between the extremes of a wholly sensationalist and a wholly non-sensationalist theory of translation there lies a possible *tertium quid*. According to this third alternative, 'Perhaps a *part* of the meaning of the relevant terms is given in sensation, while the remainder is fixed by a cluster of background beliefs.'[13] But this weaker sensationalist thesis, Churchland claims,

> ... requires us to deny that the beings with the infra-red eyes can perceive the temperature of objects, and indeed to deny that *any* beings, no matter what their sensory apparatus, can perceive the temperature of objects unless they are subject to precisely the same range of bodily sensations with which we *happen* to respond to hot and cold objects.[14]

It is far from clear, however, that this third alternative is nearly as badly off as this passage of Churchland's suggests. Nor is it clear that, to the extent that the *A/E* case *does* present problems for this third alternative, these problems are not in fact directly a function of the way our language *actually operates*. Like Sellars, though considerably less clearly, Churchland can be construed as drawing conclusions about what our language is *actually* like which rest ultimately on

---

11 Ibid., 13

12 Ibid., 11-12

13 Ibid., 12

14 Ibid., 12

arguments which can at best be taken as showing what it *would have to be* like if it were internally coherent. But it cannot be simply presupposed that our language *is* internally coherent. In fact, with respect to the meaning of observation predicates like 'is hot' and 'is white,' it is highly likely that ordinary language *is not* coherent, being torn between, on the one hand, a naive realist, and on the other hand, a (merely) causal account, of the relevant objective parameters.

Churchland is in effect forcing the third alternative to adopt the problems of the extreme sensationalist approach: the possibility of an alternative between the extremes of the wholly sensationalist and the wholly non-sensationalist views is just the possibility that facts about the intrinsic natures of our sensations play *some* (essential) role in what we mean by common observation predicates like 'is hot.' Churchland forces that role to dominate, thereby inflicting the suggested *tertium quid* with problems involved in the more radical sensationalist view. Moreover, Churchland is assuming here that understanding, and hence translation, is an all or nothing thing. But there is no justification for such an assumption. Indeed, it will be a consequence of the view which we will endorse that even between individual *E*s or individual *A*s the possibility of total understanding is extremely, if not completely, unlikely. Let's examine more closely Churchland's *A/E* argument.

III

Even 'common-sense' theories admit of levels of sophistication; and while Churchland may be right that the extreme sensationalist position which he refutes with his *A/E* case is in fact condoned by common-sense, this could, it will be argued, be true of only a very crude level of common-sense. In fact, the position which Churchland attributes to the sensationalist can easily be shown to be false without the extravagance of invoking aliens; its inadequateness is exceedingly obvious.

Expressions such as 'is hot,' and 'is white,' which are the type of expressions to which Churchland applies his *A/E* test case, are connected, in some way for which any adequate theory about the meaning of such expressions must offer an account, to expressions such as 'feels hot,' (or, in *A*, 'looks hot'), and 'looks white.' The sensationalist theory which Churchland attacks goes seriously astray in that it completely ignores, so far as the meaning of is-talk itself is concerned, the distinction between these two types of expressions. A theory about the meaning of is-talk ought to draw this distinction and attempt to disentangle the relationship between the distinguished items. Churchland's sensationalist opponent virtually collapses is-talk into looks-talk by attributing to is-talk the meaning and thus the truth conditions which a considerably more worthy sensationalist opponent would attribute only to looks-talk. In the setting up of his *A/E* case, Churchland himself clearly uses and, as will be argued in more detail later, is committed to a sensationalist analysis of, looks-talk. The claim that, on behalf of the sensationalist, he collapses is-talk into looks-talk is thus not equivalent to the claim that he doesn't see a role for looks-talk. It is rather the claim that he construes the sensationalist as attributing an *identical* role to is-talk. Why else would he insist, in his *A/E* case, that from the fact that snow *looks black* to *A*s a strong sensationalist theory of meaning must force us to translate their 'Snow is cold' as our 'Snow is black'? The sensationalist element involved in the meaning of the *E* expression 'is cold' is *controlled* in a way, which Churchland's extreme sensationalist chooses totally to ignore, by talk about *standard observers* and *standard conditions. As just simply aren't standard E observers*. In light of this, even a sophisticated sensationalist may be faced with the superficially uncomfortable possibility that the *A*s don't mean exactly the same thing as we do when we utter, each in our respective Englishes, tokens of the sentence, 'This is hot.' But only a very naive sensationalist indeed, one who takes the meaning of is-talk to be given *straightforwardly* in terms of sensations, just as that of looks-talk is more plausibly and commonly assumed to be, is committed to holding that what *A does* mean by his utterance of 'This is hot' is captured (in any way) by what *we* mean when we say 'This is white.' Just a moment's reflection, for the purposes of which the introduction of aliens is completely otiose, reveals that such a position cannot account for the meaning of is-talk; even within our own language this position would force frequent, counter-intuitive, indeed incorrect, attributions of false belief. Thus Churchland's sensationalist would be forced to claim that whenever an object *looks red* it *is red*; even when the fact of its looking red stems from some abnormality either in the observer, the viewing conditions or both. As well, of course, he would have to claim that it is red *only* if some observer is looking at it and having a sensation of red. Under conditions of darkness, in the presence of the relevant type of colour-blind individual, or in the absence of any observer, an object simply *isn't* red according to this position. That the view that an object is red if and only if it, at present, looks red to some observer fails to accord with ordinary usage is, we take it, beyond dispute. Perhaps we might, for that reason, be permitted to engage for Churchland a more worthy opponent; more worthy because considerably less crude but still not incompatible with the deliverances of 'common-sense.' Let us try to defend a possible *tertium quid*.

Traditionally, the sensationalist position, as it has appeared in the philosophical literature, fueled, of course, by 'crude intuitions supplied by common-sense,' has taken the meaning of is-talk to be given in terms of looks-talk plus talk about standard observers and standard conditions. The meaning of looks-talk, on the other hand, has traditionally been assumed to be amenable to a purely sensationalist analysis. At least this version of the sensationalist theory of meaning has the virtue of being, even if false, not as obviously false as the position which Churchland chose to refute. The version of the theory for which we will offer the outlines of a defence will, we hope, be even less crude, and thus less open to attack, than this. The position here defended will involve a holistic view of the meaning of looks- and is-talk according to which the meaning of neither class of terms can be given in any simplistic way in terms of sensation and according to which neither class of terms rests straightforwardly on the other but rather both are elements in a logical circle – are logically intertwined with, and dependent upon, each other. The crucial point, however, the point in virtue of which the position here defended could accurately be said to involve a sensationalist theory of meaning is this: Sensations will be held to play *an essential role* in the meaning of both looks- and is-talk.

One might, perhaps, want to take a strong anti-sensationalist stand even on the meaning of looks-talk and claim that even it is, as Churchland claims about the meaning of is-talk, given purely in terms of networks of beliefs; networks of beliefs about objective parameters.[15] Thus one might wish to claim that the correct interpretation of '*x* looks P to O' is:

> O has prima facie evidence available to him, via his visual apparatus, to support the claim that *x* is P.

The point of such a maneuver for a non-sensationalist, notice, is this: Any reference to the *intrinsic nature of O's evidence* for the claim that *x* is P has been studiously avoided. The non-sensationalist's claim is thus that what is meant or communicated by statements about how things look to observers *has nothing to do with* kinds of sensory experiences undergone by observers. Contrary to what a sensationalist analysis would hold, such a view holds that to say that something looks white to one is not even in part to try to communicate anything about one's sensations. (Wilfrid Sellars has made an ingenious attempt to defend such an analysis of looks-talk, the object of which is to undercut sensationalist attempts to define is-talk in terms of looks-talk. Like Churchland, however, Sellars makes an unstated and unsupported assumption that ordinary language is internally coherent, and indeed, he rests his whole argument on that assumption.)

Consider, however, as a case in which our intuitions on the meaning of looks-talk might show themselves and in which such a non-sensationalist's intuitions might be drawn toward those of his opponent, a case which bears both a relevant resemblance to but is in another relevant sense different from, Churchland's own *A*/*E* case. The case in mind is that of the colour-blind individual. Like the *A*s he has available to him, as compared to average *E*s, qualitatively different (in this case somewhat poorer) sensory information concerning a particular objective parameter. Unlike the *A*s, however, he presumably shares with the average *E* a single language. Consider as a specific example an individual who is a deuteranope – he has a type of red-green colour-blindness which causes him to experience objects which are red or green in the same way in which both he and normal individuals experience objects which are yellow. How does such an in-

15 This point is due to Gary Wedeking.

dividual reply if, pointing to a red fire engine or some green grass, we ask him: 'What colour does that look to you?'? By the proposed non-sensationalist analysis of looks-talk, he must reply: 'It looks red or green or yellow to me,' thereby meaning: 'I have prima facie evidence available to me, via my visual apparatus, to support the claim that that fire engine is either red or green or yellow.' (His prima facie evidence for the presence of each of those objective states of affairs is – unlike that of normal observers – indistinguishable from evidence for any of the others.) But wouldn't the colour-blind individual *in fact* reply that it looks yellow to him, thereby meaning that it looks the way yellow things look, both to him and to normal *E* observers? (Assuming, of course, as ordinary language always does, that problems arising from the fact of the privacy of sensation, and which exist even in the case of completely normal observers, can be either overcome or overlooked.) If all the deuteranope were concerned to communicate with his looks-statement was information about the type of objective claim to which his experiential evidence entitled him, he would restrict himself to the disjunctive claim. That he would in fact make the more specific response indicates, surely, that he is additionally concerned, in using looks-talk, to make us cognizant – if only the problem of other minds would permit! – of the intrinsic nature of his sensory experience.

Churchland, at any rate, is apparently committed to a sensationalist account of looks-talk. He uses looks-talk in setting up the *A/E* case; and he uses it in a way which presupposes a sensationalist component. Thus when Churchland says that 'so far as the intrinsic nature of their visual sensations is concerned, the world 'looks' to [*As*] much as it looks to us in black-and-white prints of pictures taken with infrared-sensitive film,'[16] it is clear that, for him, to speak of the way the world looks to *A*s or *E*s is to make essential reference to the intrinsic nature of relevant sensations. Churchland could not possibly intend otherwise since if he were to take the non-sensationalist line on looks-talk it would be simply false, *in both the A and E languages*, to say of the *A*s that snow looks black to them. *A*s do not have prima

---

16 Churchland, *Scientific Realism and the Plasticity of Mind*, 9

facie evidence available to them, via their visual apparatus, to support the claim that snow is black! Their prima facie evidence, albeit *visual,* is to the effect that snow is *cold*! Hence, on the proposed non-sensationalist analysis of looks-talk, we would be required to say, *in E,* that snow looks cold to *A*s. Just as in the case of the deuteranope, it seems clear that this is not in fact what we would say. In setting up his *A/E* case Churchland has taken advantage of the sensationalist component which looks-talk clearly has.

But what, now, of the sensationalist's claim that information about the intrinsic qualities of sensations in fact plays a central role in the meaning of *both* looks- (and feels-) and is-talk? Churchland has argued, of course, that the meaning of common observation terms, or at least of is-talk – of expressions such as 'is hot' and 'is white' – is given entirely in terms of networks of belief, to which facts about sensations, particularly facts about the intrinsic qualities of sensations, are completely irrelevant. But Churchland speaks as though it were straightforwardly clear what, in general, a network of beliefs *is,* and how, in particular, a network of beliefs can be that which is *contrasted with,* and therefore *itself devoid of,* a sensory component. That this latter *might* be the case is not, of course, obviously precluded; that it is contentious and in need of supportive argument, however, is surely beyond dispute. We hope to create (what we take to be considerable) room for doubt concerning this assumed independence of, at least in connection with common observation terms, networks of belief from information about sensations.

Churchland in this connection frequently slips back and forth between two claims: 1) The true claim that the particular sort of sensation caused in us, *E*s, by the operation of a particular parameter, must not be mistaken to be an essential property of the parameter involved; and, 2) The here-to-be-disputed claim that facts about how a particular objective parameter is sensorily detected by us, *E*s, are irrelevant to the meaning of, to our understanding of, talk about, and in particular, observation statements connected with, that same parameter.[17]

---

17 For illustrations, see *Scientific Realism and the Plasticity of Mind,* 11-12, 13,

A passage in an earlier paper, 'Two Grades of Evidential Bias' is a particularly good illustration of Churchland's tendency to move between these two claims. The passage is interesting on other grounds as well. In *Scientific Realism and the Plasticity of Mind,* Churchland uses his *A/E* test case, as has been said, in defence of the claim that sensations are irrelevant to the meaning of expressions like 'is hot,' 'is white,' etc. In 'Two Grades of Evidential Bias' he is concerned to defend only a much weaker position. He there argues only that such expressions are what he calls *intensionally-biased;* anchored, in other words, in semantic space by webs of belief. He argues, that is, that such terms are theory-laden. This is, of course, a part, but only a part, of the position for which he strives in his book. As a consequence of this lesser goal in the paper, Churchland, in the passage presently being discussed, concedes something which he could not concede in the book. And his argument to escape the force of this concession (in fact, the concession *has no force* against the claim of theory-ladenness which he was, in the paper, concerned to defend), clearly exhibits the tendency to move between the claim that how things affect us is irrelevant to the things themselves and the claim that how things affect us is irrelevant to the meaning of our talk about these things.

Churchland concedes: 'It is quite possible for a belief such as "In normal conditions, white things and only white things look like *this* to (or cause *this* kind of sensation in) normal humans," to comprise an element of some importance in a person's understanding of the term "white".' (In the context of his book, this would be a very large concession indeed. He argues: 'But that element is a belief, among other beliefs.' Of course: the meaning of is-talk is theory-laden and the belief cited is but a strand in the web. But Churchland doesn't stop there; he goes on: '[That element] is an element whose importance will vary inversely with the number of other general beliefs [the person] has involving 'white,' for the fact it expresses is no more an *essential* fact

---

15; also, in 'Two Grades of Evidential Bias,' *Philosophy of Science* **42** (1975), see 255. Churchland often speaks of the first of these two claims as being a conclusion of his A/E argument (see *Scientific Realism and the Plasticity of Mind,* 9, 12); in fact, he explicitly assumes it in setting up that argument (*Scientific Realism and the Plasticity of Mind,* 8).

about white things than is the fact that, under certain conditions, white things and only white things cause such-and-such sensations in bumblebees, or such-and-so sensations in squid.'[18] Of course they aren't essential facts about *white things as they are in themselves*; i.e., they aren't essential facts about the objective parameter, white. But in what way does this detract from the importance of facts about our sensations in the meaning, *for us*, (not bumble bees or squid!) of talk about things being white?

In *Scientific Realism and the Plasticity of Mind*, where Churchland wants facts about sensations in observers to be not just *inessential*, but *irrelevant* to the meanings of observation terms in the observers languages, he doesn't make any concessions about the role of sensations. His illegitimate move between the two claims being discussed is thus even more obvious. Thus compare the following passage from *Scientific Realism and the Plasticity of Mind* with the passage from 'Two Grades of Evidential Bias' which was just discussed. Churchland says, '... the intrinsic qualitative identity of one's sensations is irrelevant to what properties one can or does perceive the world as displaying.' This is a version of the true claim contained in (1). Churchland goes on, as though restating the same point, or perhaps as though making a new but logically entailed point: 'The meaning of a term (or the identity of a concept) is not determined by the intrinsic quality of whatever sensation happens to prompt its observational use, but by the network of assumptions/beliefs/principles in which it figures.'[19] But the latter is, we contend, neither the same nor a logically entailed point. It is equivalent to the claim contained in (2), a quite different claim; and it is, immediately hereafter, to be disputed. Along with it, the claim that what we *are*, properly conceived, is 'epistemic engines' will be implicitly disputed as well.

Consider the plausibility of the following scenario: The participants in an Intergalactic Philosophy Conference are beginning to assemble. An *E* emerging from the crowd gathered around the coffee urn disappointedly mumbles that the coffee is cold. An *A* replies, 'So

---

18 Churchland, 'Two Grades of Evidential Bias,' 255

19 Churchland, *Scientific Realism and the Plasticity of Mind*, 15

what?' and pours himself a coffee. Everyone laughs. At one of the first conferences they'd ever had together they'd worked out the meaning of is-talk. They all appreciated the fact that there was an aspect of the meaning of the *E*'s utterance which the *A*s could, in a sense appreciate, and to that extent incorporate into their own system of meanings, but which, without some change in their sensory repertoire, they could never truly share. That the coffee was cold had a significance for the *E*s which it *did not have* for the *A*s. What was communicated to *E*s by the statement that the coffee was cold, and thus an essential part of the meaning of that statement, was something about the kinds of sensory experiences the coffee would occasion in them.

The point is not a trivial one. Indeed it is doubtful if it could be more fundamental. It is, we submit, the fact that (at least some) sensations have what we will call *'intrinsic meaning'* that underwrites the phenomenon of meaning connections as it exists in conscious beings. It is this type of 'programming' which we have and which (so far at least) computers lack: We are subject to sensations which often have *meaning* or *value* in and of themselves; they feel nice or they hurt, or, for more complex ones, they're comforting or distressing, interesting or boring, and so on. It is a lack of such intrinsically meaningful sensations (and feelings) which separates mere computers from conscious beings; and, we are suggesting, it is this lack of sensations which cuts mere computers off from having what has become known in the current debate about artificial intelligence as 'original intentionality.' Being incapable of experiences which are intrinsically meaningful, mere computers are incapable of any but so-called 'borrowed' meaning connections – the term is misleading, however, since not only are their meanings never anything but our meanings, but their meanings are meaningful only for us!

We wish to suggest even further, that it is the intrinsic meaning of sensations that accounts for our motivation to build theories about, to learn about, objective parameters in the first place. It is our desire to maximize the frequency of pleasant sensations and to minimize the frequency of unpleasant ones, which motivates us to extract patterns from and impose structure on, to postulate objective parameters as causally responsible for, the flow of our sensations.

Churchland's claim that the 'intrinsic qualitative identity' of sensations is irrelevant to the meaning of is-talk leaves him without a story to tell about why the statement that the coffee is cold means something to an average *E* which it doesn't mean to *A*s. But much worse, in claiming that sensations are mere causal middle-men which might ultimately be dispensed with entirely, he cuts himself off from the account, albeit a 'mere psychological' one, but nevertheless *the only one we have,* of our motivation to construct theories at all. What Churchland confuses is the fact that no *particular* set of sensations is necessarily related to the objective parameters with the fact that *some* sensations must play the explanatory role in order to have an account of the role of theories at all. He mistakes, that is, the fact that no particular psychology of sensation is necessarily true for the one that no psychology of sensation is necessary. We have been suggesting that some psychology of sensation *is* necessary, *both* for its causal role *and* for its intrinsic, qualitative content.

IV

The point can be expanded and deepened by considering another argument of Churchland's. In *Scientific Realism and the Plasticity of Mind,* he uses an extended discussion of our common-sense theory of heat and cold to illustrate how the fact that the observation predicates involved in that theory are themselves hopelessly theory-laden serves to undermine '[t]he conviction that the world instantiates our ordinary observation predicates.' Such a conviction, he argues, just 'cannot be defended by a simple appeal to the "manifest deliverances of sense." '[20] While readily conceding Churchland's theory-ladenness claim and with it the fallibility of simple observation as a test of the appropriateness of observation predicates, we would like to illustrate how this does not, in fact cannot, amount to conceding the conclusion of Churchland's *A/E* argument. It does not and cannot amount to accepting the thesis that facts about the intrinsic qualities of sensations are irrelevant to the meaning of common observation predicates like 'is hot.'

---

20 Ibid., 24

Churchland shows how we are initially driven to hold a belief in the operation of an additional objective parameter such as heat conductivity by the occurrence of phenomena incompatible with our belief in the operation of a single simple objective parameter such as temperature: An object, A, feels warmer to the touch than a second object, B; placed in contact with one another, however, A is caused to warm up, to feel warmer to the touch than it did before contact. If we were to accept, as Churchland says we common-sensically do, (1) the idea that feeling warmer is the same as being warmer, (2) the idea that the fact of an object causing another object to warm up indicates a greater degree of warmth in the first object, as well as, (3) the general principle that if an object is warmer than a second the second is not warmer than the first, then our empirical findings would have to be acknowledged as being in conflict with the general principle given in (3). We postulate a parameter, heat conductivity, or rate of exchange of heat energy from one body to another, to explain this set of phenomena: B must be warmer than A (it has a higher degree of heat energy), because it causes A to warm up; but A must be a better heat conductor because it feels warmer to the touch than does B – it passes heat energy to our hand more efficiently than does B. The question, now, is this: What does talk about heat conductivity, what do expressions like 'is a good conductor of heat', mean? And the answer is that, if we are to know what the claim 'A is a better conductor of heat than B' means, we must know facts like: A will feel warmer to the touch than B when B has an equal (or even somewhat greater) degree of heat than A; or: A container made out of substance A will allow a hot liquid to cool off faster than will a container made out of substance B; or: An object made out of substance A will become hot quicker when exposed to a source of heat than will an object made out of substance B; facts, that is, of the sort which drove us to postulate the parameter in the first place. Churchland calls collections of facts like these 'networks of beliefs' and he thinks that they totally determine the meaning, at the 'common-sense' (in this case the improved common-sense) level, of is-talk. He's *right* about that. He also thinks, however, that these networks of belief determine the meaning of is-talk *independently of sensations*. But each strand in these networks of belief involves essential reference, implicit perhaps, but essential nonetheless, to sensations. The reference is explicit in the first example given above. A will *feel warmer* than B. It's implicit in the other two but there just the same. In both cases the content of the claims is going to have to be spelled out in terms of how things will look and/or feel to observers.

That we could have, as Churchland has shown, gotten at the same objective parameters through different kinds of sensory experiences might be thought to show that though sensations are essentially involved in networks of belief, their *intrinsic qualitative natures* are themselves irrelevant to meaning. The role of sensations would then be open to the purely causal analysis which Churchland, following Sellars, would favour. But such a view of meaning is surely too implausible. Surely our system of meanings is a tool fitted to serve our needs and interests – quite irrespective of however 'narrow' and 'parochial' those needs and interests might appear to be from any point of view but our own! Surely what is contained in, and communicated by, the meaning of our terms is *what matters to us*. If not, how could we account for the purpose, and hence even the existence, of meaning in particular, and of theory in general? It is the intrinsic nature of sensations which leads us to decide against using materials which are known to be good heat conductors in the making of handles for cooking utensils. If to learn that some substance is a good conductor of heat is to learn something which implies that we should not use it to make handles for cooking utensils, this is presumably because not only facts about sensations but facts about the intrinsic natures of sensations are communicated by, and are essentially involved in the meaning of, is-talk.

It should be clear from the foregoing that a proponent of the sensationalist theory of meaning is not precluded, as Churchland implies, from holding a belief in the possibility that our common-sense conceptual framework, and with it our common-sense observation predicates, such as 'is hot,' 'is hotter than ____,' *is theoretical* and might eventually be eliminated, even for the purposes of ordinary discourse, in favour of a more powerful, more empirically adequate, conceptual framework. But on the sensationalist position the elimination of a conceptual framework – neither of a low-level, common-sense one nor of a high order scientific one (Churchland and the rest are right: the two are on a continuum and of a kind) – does not thereby eliminate the sensory core which is, for the sensationalist, an essential component in the meaning of all observation terms. Rather, what is in essence the same sensory core, expanded perhaps, or differently divided or interrelated, is incorporated into the new, more powerful conceptual framework. Thus the possibility of the elimination of the common-sense framework is not, alas, the possibility which the materialist needs and wants.

Our common-sense theory of perception might, as Churchland claims, be false, ('or even seriously superficial'[21]), but it isn't false because of a failure to appreciate that it is totally theoretical and of a failure to purge it of all sensory content. Rather the problem is that *not enough* information about, and/or enough systematization and interpretation of information about, sensations has been worked into the theory. The fact that several objective parameters can conspire in different combinations to account for the occurrence in various cases of a single type of sensation, or, as in the *A/E* case, that the same objective parameter can be causally responsible for different sensations, does not imply that we could ever cut information about sensations out of the meaning of talk about objective parameters.

V

One final point: Churchland speaks of us as 'talking measuring instruments,"[22]; as '[standing] rather badly in need of wholesale recalibration';[23] and of the possibility of sensations, as mere '*causal* middle-men,' being bypassed, 'dispensed with,' entirely.[24] The 'ideal epistemic engine' which he envisages, or at least dreams of, for the future will be a perfectly calibrated instrument totally efficient at 'pulling information from the environment.'[25] Surely the picture is one of

21 Ibid., 6

22 Ibid., 40

23 Ibid., 41

24 Ibid., 15

25 Ibid., 150

leaving behind our 'crude' conception of ourselves as thinking, feeling, sensing organisms and assuming our rightful place at the pinnacle of the class of thinking machines. Surely, that is, when our 'common-sense "theory of persons" '[26] is rejected, *feelings* will go the way of sensations. Feelings, like sensations, will undoubtedly be properly seen as states of our physiological systems. It's interesting, then, that when it serves his purposes Churchland helps himself to feelings: He speaks of 'much beauty and endless intrigue [rewarding] the determined observer,' and of the 'satisfaction of apprehending reality, perceptually, in ways that reflect more deeply and accurately the structure and content of that reality… '[27] Such lapses are simply unavoidable. Feelings, like sensations, are the privilege of conscious beings and not of *mere* epistemic engines. Feelings, like sensations, possess intrinsic qualitative content and thus feelings, like sensations are the source of the motivation which a conscious being requires if he is to construct theories – or indeed – if he is to do anything at all. Irrespective of however great a hurdle it might represent for the scientific comprehension of conscious beings, it is simply a fact that feelings and sensations play an ineliminable role in the production of the behaviour of such beings. Feelings and sensations, with their *intrinsic qualitative content*, are the source of meaning in our lives and hence ultimately are the source of meaning in our language. Churchland, like the rest of us, is, in his unguarded moments, fully appreciative of this fact, as his remarks about feelings demonstrate.

Received July, 1983
Revised March, 1984

26 Ibid., 5

27 Ibid., 36

CANADIAN JOURNAL OF PHILOSOPHY
Supplementary Volume 11

On the Speculative Nature of Our Self Conception: A Reply to Some Criticisms

PAUL M. CHURCHLAND
University of California, San Diego
La Jolla, CA 92093

I must begin by thanking the editors for offering me the opportunity to respond to two of the other papers in this collection: 'A Materialist's Misgivings about Eliminative Materialism,' by Jeff Foss; and 'Sensation, Theory, and Meaning,' by Bonnie Thurston and Sam Coval. In some earlier publications I have defended eliminative materialism at some length (1981, 1984), and in others I have argued that the semantics of common observation terms is exhausted by their inferential or conceptual role, to the exclusion of any purely phenomenological component (1975, 1979). Foss criticizes the first thesis; Thurston and Coval, the second. I propose to defend both.

I. Eliminative Materialism

It is convenient to address Jeff Foss's criticisms first. Foss and I already share a good number of the relevant premises here. We are both materialists; we both regard the common-sense conceptual framework of 'folk psychology' as a speculative and corrigible causal/explanatory theory of the behaviour and inner workings of *homo sapiens*; and we both regard the elimination of that theory's ontology, on broadly empirical grounds, as something that is, at least in principle, *possible*.

What Foss wants to know is, where are the decisive or compelling empirical grounds for believing *now* that folk psychology (not just could, but) *will* suffer wholesale elimination at the hands of a matured neuroscience, rather than enjoy a successful intertheoretic reduction of some sort or other? My answer is that there are no decisive, or even very compelling, grounds for expecting a blanket elimination of the ontology of folk psychology. Blanket elimination of its entire ontology, as Foss points out, is but the left-most position on a broad spectrum of intertheoretic possibilities, a spectrum that also includes varying degrees of partial elimination, and/or varying degrees of conceptual revision of old concepts. If decisive evidence, now, for the extreme case is what we are looking for, then I agree with Foss that we must currently go disappointed.

Dialectically, however, this criticism is not very interesting since, as Foss himself complains, defenders of an eliminativism of that strength and confidence are surpassingly hard to find. What one does find is a more cautious and sensible breed. Some of us are willing to advance the less extreme position that there already exists a body of modestly compelling empirical evidence for expecting that current and future developments in both psychology and neuroscience will lead to major conceptual revisions in folk psychology, and to the outright elimination of at least some parts of its ontology. Accordingly, I shall argue further, we would be methodologically derelict not to *encourage* the active pursuit of theoretical approaches to cognitive activity that owe nothing to the ontology and presumptions of common sense.

I am happy to admit, however, that the evidence against folk psychology is diffuse, ambiguous, and scattered, and that even reasonable people can disagree on how great its damage, and how dark its portent. We are dealing, after all, with a large-scale theoretical issue, an issue that will be decided by the cumulative effect of a great many considerations, and not by a single empirical bullet. One's estimate of the situation of folk psychology will depend heavily on the details and the structure of the network of assumptions one brings to the issue. My basic aim in the first half of this paper is to try to defend, and to make intelligible for the reader, the empirical and theoretical rationale that underwrites a fairly strong scepticism concerning the future of folk psychology.

I begin the defense by contrasting my rationale with the one Foss offers. For Foss, eliminative materialism (EM) first recommended itself as a source of relief from a certain embarrassment he felt as a materialist: the embarrassment of not yet being able to offer adequate reductive accounts of such things as consciousness and sensory qualia. But these felt materialist inadequacies could be suppressed, and the reductive obligation could be side-stepped, Foss perceived, if one could simply deny the existence of the troublesome explanatory targets. On this reconstruction, EM emerges as a merely expedient means for Foss to avoid discharging a large and legitimate obligation, a (fleeting and uncharacteristic) dereliction of intellectual duty for which his current paper is public atonement.

These were indeed poor reasons for embracing EM. They are not and never have been my reasons. I came to EM slowly, and belatedly, after having been a materialist (first an identity theorist, and then a functionalist) for over a decade. I was moved towards EM not by the feeling that the resources of materialistic neuroscience were in any way inadequate to account for human cognitive phenomena, but by the increasing feeling that our *folk psychological* conceptions, of the very phenomena to be explained, were systematically inadequate to and perhaps even positively misrepresented the facts to be explained.

I had never felt any embarrassment at my current inability to provide an acceptable reductive account of, say, the wondrous qualities displayed by our olfactory sensations, because the phenomenon was obviously both complex and subtle; the systematic unravelling of the brain had only just begun; and the background presumption in favour of the truth of materialism – as derived from evolutionary theory, developmental embryology, biology, and neurophysiology – seemed absolutely overwhelming. There was simply no reason for embarrassment: the resources available were enormous, and these things take time.

EM thus held no particular appeal for me. Certainly I found it a deeply intriguing theoretical suggestion, but I saw little empirical motive for embracing it, and I felt no dialectical pressures that made it appear as a refuge.

So what happened to my orthodox and conservative materialism in the philosophy of mind? Three things. The first occurred in epistemology. By 1972 I had begun to despair of the orthodox philosophical approaches to the problem of the rational evolution of knowledge structures. In particular, I was led to doubt the basic kinematical ideal that knowledge was adequately represented by a set of sentences, and the basic dynamical idea that what drives and determines changes in our knowledge is the set of logical and quasi-logical relations holding on that set of sentences.

Many things motivated this doubt. The massive failure of the Hypothetico-Deductive and Bayesian accounts of learning, for all but 'toy' universes. The fact that using and manipulating sets of sentential attitudes is itself something that is learned. And the fact that the vast majority of learning in the biological kingdom, now and over the last 100 million years, has taken place without the benefit of anything remotely resembling sets of sentences. Sentential attitudes and their mutual relations, I concluded, fail to represent the basic kinematical elements and dynamical factors that constitute our evolving knowledge of the world. They may be the central elements in folk psychology, but they are at best a superficial reflection of what is really going on.

The second rush of considerations was almost entirely empirical. By 1976, my wife and colleague, Patricia Churchland, had launched herself on a systematic course of study in the neurosciences, and this included a weekly study tour ('grand rounds') of the changing population of patients in the neurology ward of a major urban hospital. She thus began her acquaintance (and through her, so did I) with the wide variety of physical traumas to which human brains are subject, and with the unexpected and bewildering variety of cognitive, affective, perceptual, and motor deficits which these traumas produce.

What was striking was that the syndromes observed were so often sharply paradoxical. To cite just three quick examples, there were patients who were stony (cortically) blind, but who emphatically denied their deficit and freely confabulated excuses for their clumsy behavior and clear test failures ('blindness denial'). They were blind but did not know it. Other patients had lost all visual sensation through the loss of their visual cortex, and quite properly insisted that they were blind, but were able to 'guess' the position of flashing lights with almost perfect accuracy ('blind sight'). They were blind, but still could see. Still other subjects would cease to respond to, or acknowledge in any way, the existence of the entire left half of their perceptual and motor universe, and would sincerely deny ownership of, for example, their left arm and leg ('hemi-neglect'). Other syndromes fractured some 'unitary' cognitive faculty (memory, sight, language, or consciousness) into a surprising number of unexpectedly discreet and disconnected sub-faculties, some of which survived and some of which had been destroyed. Still other syndromes involved manias, dementias, and diffuse cognitive catastrophes that defy easy summary.

The list was a long one, the variety seemed endless, and its cumulative effect was quite unnerving. A neurology ward stands to folk psychology as near-luminous velocities stand to Newtonian Mechanics, as very large masses stand to Newton's gravitational theory, and as very high or very low pressures stand to the classical gas law. That is to say, when applied to phenomena outside the comfortable bubble of 'familiar' cases, the categorial and explanatory resources of the old theory quickly prove feckless and impotent. The old theory looked as good as it did, initially, only because our attention was confined to a very narrow subset of the relevant phenomena.

These historical parallels seemed ominous, since the resolution of all of these crises involved major conceptual change and ontological revision. Respectively, we lost Newtonian mass, gravitational force, and caloric fluid from our scientific ontology. And the theories that replaced them embodied a startlingly different view of the reality at issue: relativistic mass, curved spacetime, and the chaotic motion of trillions of molecules. I began seriously to believe that a similar pattern was in the process of unfolding for folk psychology.

This growing scepticism was further fanned by the empirical results of Nisbett and Wilson (1977), and Nisbett and Ross (1980), which were also brought to my attention by Patricia Churchland.

These results show that, even in the case of normal humans, the explanations we spontaneously and non-mendaciously offer, in explanation of our choices or beliefs or behaviours, regularly have no basis at all in introspection; rather, they are confabulated on the spot, and on grounds little or no different from those which sustain our third-person explanations. Even our 'introspection,' it seems, is substantially a matter of forced interpretation.

The third and final set of considerations began to emerge as, in 1980, I undertook my own education in the neurosciences, working in the CNS lab of Larry Jordan, learning the microstructure of the brain, and exploring theories about the functional basis of the 'wiring' found in this or that neural module. The details of this undertaking are the hardest of all to summarize, but their collective effect was to loosen the grip on my imagination held by the explanatory framework of folk psychology. As I learned about the brain's physical architecture, and as I learned various new theories of the computational activities that it could sustain, I gradually became comfortable in the idea that there really *were* quite general ways of representing cognitive activity that made no use of intentional idioms or deductive logic. Once real conceptual alternatives had begun to present themselves, and to compete for explanatory space, the assembled idioms of folk psychology began to look like just another face in the crowd. (For a sympathetic presentation of one of the most promising of these theoretical approaches, see Churchland [1985b].)

There was nothing essentially *eliminative* about these latter reflections, but in conjunction with the earlier considerations, they certainly helped to grease the slippery slope. They also recalled a piece of methodological advice advanced by Paul Feyerabend (1963), which counselled that the most effective way to discover the important empirical inadequacies in an old and deeply entrenched theory is to construct alternative theories with which to provide entirely *new* interpretations of the old and familiar empirical data. Any theory quite properly suppresses a good deal of empirical evidence as irrelevant and inevitable 'noise.' If the theory is deeply wrong, however, the only way to identify relevant and refuting signal in that 'noise' is by actively exploring alternative theoretical approaches that owe absolutely nothing to the entrenched framework. This I resolved to do. I have been pursuing cognitive neurobiology ever since. Some recent results of that research appear in Churchland (1985b).

The preceding account does not show that the ontology of folk psychology is a blanket illusion. Rather, it sketches the rationale for a certain methodological approach to cognitive theory, an approach that is deliberately sceptical about the integrity of folk psychology. The alternative, it seems to me, is a deeply unjustified complacency, a complacency to which Foss seems to have succumbed. Let me close this section with some replies to his more specific criticisms.

Foss complains that EM is 'promisory note philosophy.' So indeed it is. But it is no less so than is the reductive materialism preferred by Foss. The identity theory predicts that a matured neuroscience will successfully reduce folk psychology. That is at least as presumptuous a projection as that of EM. In fact, it is decidedly more presumptuous, as I have argued before (Churchland, 1984, 47). Foss resists this claim (in note 32), but I say he misrepresents the alternatives. If 'M' represents the truth of materialism, and 'F' the truth of folk psychology, then the identity theory claims that (M & F), while EM claims that (M & ∼F). The a priori probability of these, claims Foss, is the same.

I disagree. To apply the principle of indifference to F and ∼F is to ignore the fact that ∼F hides a legion of relevant possibilities. Folk psychology is but one possible theory out of millions of incompatible competitors, and the *a priori* probability of F is not .5, as Foss alleges, but something negligibly different from zero. The a priori probability of (M & F) is therefore also at the vanishing point. A priori, EM has a vast advantage over the identity theory.

The all-up *posterior* probability of F, to be sure, is much higher than zero, since folk psychology boasts at least some successes. But we must also consider the explanatory failures, sketched above, and at greater length in my (1981), which suggest that it is false. My guess would put the posterior probability of folk psychology no higher than .25, and whatever its value, it is falling.

Foss rejects my complaints concerning the explanatory failures of folk psychology, replying that current neuroscience has little more to say about such cases than does folk psychology. I could reply that this is not true, and launch into neurophysiological detail. Or I could reply that this charge is irrelevant, since the eventual explanatory *success* of the neurosciences is an assumption shared by both parties to this debate (the reductionist and the eliminativist). Either response would be sufficient. But it is more germane to make the Feyerabendean reply that it takes *time* to put together a good theory. Folk psychology has had three thousand years to repair its deficits, without visible motion forward. Fairness demands that our fast-moving neuroscience be given at least a century or two.

My arguments here, in support of conducting research on the working assumption that elimination is the destiny of much of folk psychology, do not preclude our being delighted if and when we do stumble upon the occasional reductive opportunity. Reduction is always desirable, if you can get it. And no doubt some of folk psychology will be successfully reduced. (Foss cites, as especially demanding of reductive explanation, the qualitative character of our sensations. Here, I believe, he will get his wish. At the end of the next section, I outline just such a reductive explanation – for visual, gustatory, and olfactory sensations – in terms of neurally embodied phase spaces.)

However, to proceed on the assumption that of course folk psychology will reduce, and to make it a requirement on theories in cognitive neurobiology that they address and explain the categorial framework of folk psychology, would be to blinker one's theoretical imagination at the outset, and to deflect research from the very areas that might set us free. It would make new theories answer not to the facts, but to an already entrenched *theory*. This is a bad idea at any time. And it is an especially bad idea in the case of a theory as troubled as folk psychology.

II. The Semantic, Epistemological and Ontological Status of Sensations

Thurston and Coval have a three-stage agenda: semantics, epistemology, and ontology. Very briefly, they wish to retain a residual semantic role for sensations, in order to retain a certain minimal kind of phenomenological foundation in epistemology. And they appeal to this epistemological position in turn, in order to short circuit any attempts to provide a purely physical account of our conscious cognitive activities. Let me take the stages of their argument in sequence.

Thurston and Coval (hereafter, T & C) certainly concede much of what I was concerned to establish in ch. 2 of my (1979). They agree that our observation predicates are irredeemably laden with theory. They agree that the meaning of such terms is substantially fixed by the set of general beliefs in which they figure. They appear to agree that term-synonomy across speakers is a matter of sharing roughly the same set of beliefs in which the term at issue is embedded. And they explicitly agree that it is not an essential feature of external parameters such as warmth or redness, but a merely *contingent* feature, that they typically cause in us sensations of a certain character.

All of this entails that two biologically different creatures could typically respond to the same objective property *F* through different sensory modalities and with quite different sensations, and yet converse relevantly and fluently with each other about that same objective property, so differently detected by each.

Nevertheless, insist T & C, there would be a residual difference in the meaning that '*F* had for each creature. For included among the general beliefs that constitute their understandings of the term '*F* is a belief of the form '*F* things typically cause a sensation of kind S in creatures of my type.' But the qualitative character S is something quite *different* for creatures of each type, and so we have a (minor) difference in the meaning of '*F* for each of the two types of creature.

It is perhaps true, concede T & C, that the idiosyncratic qualitative character of one's sensations is irrelevant to whether one can *perceive* whether external objects are *F*, since any type of sensation will do, so long as it is causally connected in the right ways. But the having of *some* sensation or other is surely essential, and for each speaker the peculiar character of his sensation will inevitably enter, via the kind of belief mentioned, as one of the elements in his understanding of the term '*F*.' Sensational differences across creatures will therefore yield corresponding meaning differences, of small but non-zero magnitude. It is therefore a mistake for me to claim that 'the meaning of the relevant observation terms has nothing to do with the intrinsic qualitative identity of whatever sensations just happen to prompt their non-inferential application in singular empirical judgements.' (1979, 11)

I wish to dispute both of the major elements of this counter thesis: (a) that some sensaton or other is surely essential to any case of observational knowledge, and (b) that variation in such sensations across speakers entails differences in the meanings of the predicates whose application they prompt. Let me address (b) first.

In my (1975) paper, cited by T & C, I conceded that a belief such as, 'Under normal circumstances, red things cause sensations of kind R in me,' could constitute a significant element in a given person's *understanding* of the term 'red.' (I then went on to argue that this element was nonetheless an undistinguished member of a large set of beliefs, and reflected no essential connection between the sensation and the colour in any case.) T & C seize on this concession as being in flat contradiction with the position I take in my (1979) book, where I argue that the qualitative character of sensations is entirely irrelevant to the *meaning* of common observation terms. Prima facie, these claims do indeed appear to be in conflict, but in fact I am innocent of the charge of self-contradiction.

In section 8 of my (1979), a section explicitly entitled 'Meaning and Understanding,' I motivate and explicate a careful distinction between an individual's *understanding* of a term T, and the *meaning* of T within a given linguistic community. As I there define them, these notions are very different. The former is defined only for individuals, and is given by the set of accepted sentences that are systemically important for that individual. The latter is defined only for a community collectively, and is given by the set of sentences, containing T, that are semantically important for that community. The contrast between systemic and semantic importance is there also explained.

As applied to the case at issue, the idea is roughly as follows. The idiosyncratic character of one's sensations may indeed enter into an individual's idiosyncratic understanding of a given observation term, but it does not enter into the objective, public meaning of that term, which abstracts from such publicly inaccessible and dynamically unimportant details. Whether or not it is true, this position is entirely consistent, and was carefully constructed to be so.

In the much discussed case of the aliens who see temperatures with infrared eyes, versus we humans who feel temperatures with our fingers, the case for translating their 'temperature' vocabulary straightforwardly into our own temperature vocabulary seemed to me in 1979, and still seems to me now, to be overwhelming. That fact seemed sufficient grounds for claiming that our respective meanings were the same. Since our sensations were, ex hypothesis, very different, I concluded that the qualitative character of our sensations must have nothing to do with meanings.

In fact, we should notice, T & C conclude much the same thing. They, too, recommend that the best translation is the straightforward homophonic one, not because our respective meanings are exactly the same, but because on their view they are *almost* exactly the same, and nothing else comes closer. From which they conclude that the qualitative character of sensations has (only) a small and residual contribution to meanings.

Why are we arguing about this residual difference? I have already advanced and defended an account of meaning (1979, ch. 3) which allows us to count this residuum as too small to constitute a difference in meaning, but I can quite easily imagine T & C finding fault with any theory of meaning that has this consequence. What hangs on this issue? Why is it important to T & C to salvage a residual semantic role for sensations, however reduced and enfeebled it might be?

It is important for them, I conjecture, because so long as the semantic importance of sensations turns out to be something other than zero, then they are still in a position to claim that the existence of some sensations or other is absolutely essential to the process of empirical knowledge in humans. Such sensations constitute, for T & C, a sine qua non of real consciousness. They can serve as the distinguishing feature of true conscious cognition as against the empty simulations that AI might produce. And they form a major barrier to the reduction of genuine cognitive activity to the merely physical activities in the brain. We are not, T & C insist, mere 'epistemic engines.'

I will close this essay by arguing two theses. First, that sensations are not essential for empirical knowledge, neither semantically or epistemologically. And second, that even if they were essential, they are in any case entirely reducible, qualia and all, to the categories of cognitive neurobiology.

The first thesis has already been argued at length in print, first by Paul Feyerabend (1969), and later by myself (1982). The thrust of the argument consists in constructing an imaginary case in which the information-carrying causal chains that lead to the production of one's singular empirical judgments are re-routed so as to exclude the sensations that are normally a part of the chain. Our judgments end up with the same distal connections to the external world, but by way of different proximal elements. The point of this Gedankenexperiment is that our cognitive access to the world would be impoverished not at all. So long as spontaneous empirical judgments were caused to occur with the same frequency and accuracy they display when caused by sensations, then the adventure of empirical knowledge could go on much as in our own case. An inner domain of qualitative states to which we have direct introspective access is a colourful idiosyncracy, perhaps, but hardly an essential feature of empirical cognition.

We may anticipate that T & C will reject the imagined case as having already fallen outside the limits of genuine conscious cognition, as being something that a phenomenologically empty robot might realize, but not a conscious human. This is not a productive line to take, I suggest, since the type of case described is not science fictional. Neurology wards already provide us with partial examples of what I have described.

The phenomenon, briefly mentioned earlier, is called 'blind sight,' and it has the following character. Among subjects who are cortically blind, from suffering the loss of one or both halves of their visual cortex at the rear of the brain, there is a complete cessation of visual sensations in one or both of their hemi-fields. They pronounce themselves blind, that is, in one or both halves of their visual field. And yet somehow they can visually detect the position of a blinking light placed in the 'blind' hemi-field. They insist that they see nothing whatever, but they can 'guess' the position of the light with an accuracy of close to 100 percent.

This phenomenon is perhaps not utterly mysterious. Though their visual cortex may be destroyed, and with it the machinery for sustaining the familiar run of visual sensations, these subjects retain a distinct and phylogenetically older visual system in the midbrain called the superior colliculus. Its function in normal subjects is to detect sudden changes or movements within the visual field so as to direct the eyes to make a reflexive saccade to foveate the unusual stimulus. It has the capacity to register the kind of positional information to which the blind-sight patients are somehow responding. The retinal information thus appears to make its way to the centers of judgment by this older route through the midbrain. Or so it is conjectured. What is interesting is that this older route, though quite reliable, seems not to involve any kind of visual sensations whatever. We thus have the prompting of reliable empirical judgments, but without sensations. And we have it in real, live, cognizing humans. Sensations, it seems, are not only dispensible in principle; they are dispensible in fact.

Conceivably, everything I have said here is wrong. Conceivably, sensations are an ineliminable part of both the semantics and the epistemology of empirical judgments. But even if they were, the anti-materialist conclusions that T & C wish to draw from this would remain profoundly unwarranted, because whatever their semantic and epistemological role, sensations themselves promise to fit very neatly indeed into a materialist account of mind.

Recent theoretical developments in neuroscience suggest a general and unexpectedly powerful account of the various qualia displayed in our several sensory modalities. I now propose to outline this account. The point is to illustrate, not just the abstract possibility of a neurophysiological reduction of sensory qualia, but the outlines of what may prove to be the *actual* route of reduction for these 'ineffable' features.

I begin at one remove from sensations: at the problem of objective colour as a feature of physical objects. And I recall to your attention Edwin Land's (1977) theory of objective colour. Each object has a certain reflectance efficiency (between 0 and 100%) at three critical wavelengths in the electromagnetic spectrum, the three wavelengths that correspond to the maximal sensitivities of the three types of cones in our retinas. The colour of an object, runs the theory, is just its peculiar triplet of reflectance values. Land illustrates his theory with a three-dimensional coordinate space, a colour 'cube,' one corner of which represents reflectances of (0, 0, 0), and the diametrically opposite corner of which represents reflectances of (100, 100, 100). Every colour perceivable by the human visual system is represented by a unique position within this cube. Black is at (0, 0, 0). White is at (100, 100, 100). Mid-grey is at (50, 50, 50). And at points away from this main diagonal across the cube reside every colour known to man.

Let us now move inside the brain, and address the problem of accounting for the qualia of our visual sensations. Consider an entirely standard, three-dimensional coordinate space or phase space whose three axes x, y, z represent the spiking frequencies in a special triplet of neural pathways in the human brain. We can represent any state of activation of that neural system (a triplet of spiking frequencies) by a single *point* in the corresponding 3-D coordinate space. In the case of visual perception, each spiking frequency is an internal representation of the intrinsic reflectance of an external object at a certain wavelength. The assembled triplet of frequencies represents the object's intrinsic objective colour. And that triplet of spiking frequencies *constitutes* a sensation – a sensation, as we say, *of* that colour. Each point in the second 3-D space described represents a unique triplet, and thus a unique visual sensation. It is a 'qualia cube,' or a 'qualia phase space.'

A maximal frequency on all three pathways constitutes a sensation of white. A minimal frequency on all three pathways constitutes a sensation of black. And the many possible combinations of intermediate frequencies constitute the entire panoply of colour sensations possible for the human visual system, including sensations of the many nonspectral colours, such as brown, gold, vermillion, and day-glo orange. Moreover, *similarity* of sensations emerges quite naturally as a matter of the spatial *proximity* of their respective points in phase space. This allows us to make quantitative sense of the notion of *degrees* of similarity between sensations, and even of the various dimensions along which we can sensibly measure such degrees.

We have yet to identify the cortical machinery that embodies this functional scheme, but the retina's triune cone system, which projects to the visual cortex, offers real empirical encouragement. And such a simple system buys a substantial volume of representational capacity at a very low price. If each 'axis' of the system admits of only ten significantly different spiking frequencies (significantly different from the point of view of the downstream brain systems to which they connect), then the system will successfully distinguish 10^3 different colours. Increasing the degrees of discrimination along each axis of course raises the discriminatory volume of the system sharply.

A similar strategy may well be used by our gustatory system, although here the relevant phase space must have four dimensions, since that is the number of distinct taste-receptors (the so-called sweet, sour, salt, and bitter receptors) on the human tongue. Any taste sensation possible for humans therefore resides, I suggest, at some point within a four-dimensional gustatory phase space. This does not entail the implausible view that the taste of the fabled Australian Vegemite is somehow a 'mixture' of these four taste sensations. It entails, rather, that each of those four 'simple' sensations is a still a *quadruple* of spiking frequencies, three of which frequencies have the value zero. The taste of Vegemite, I presume (never having tasted it), is just an unusual quadruple of non-zero frequencies. This view also entails that, if our discrimination along each axis is equal to our discrimination along each axis of visual phase, then the variety of possible taste sensations probably exceeds the variety of possible colour sensations by something close to an order of magnitude. And thus it seems.

Olfactory sensations yield smoothly to much the same sort of story. Here the variety of different receptors is unclear, but is generally thought to be at least six. Every humanly possible olfactory sensation, I therefore conjecture, consists in a sextuple of spiking frequencies in a proprietary set of pathways in the forebrain's olfactory bulb, and can be represented by a unique point in a six-dimensional phase space. Assuming discrimination along each axis comparable to the other modalities, a 6-D phase space has an enormous volume — 10^6 cells — and will permit extraordinary feats of discrimination and recognition. With even finer discrimination along each axis, the functional volume explodes as the sixth power of the increase. Presumably we have here the explanation of the amazing olfactory capacities of the canines, who can discriminate, it is said, between any two of the 3.5 billion people on the planet.

Here then is a sketch of a substantive reductionist program which accounts for the continous variety of sensations in each of several different modalities, for the network of similarity relations that unite the sensations within in each modality, and even for the relative differences in the number of distinct sensations displayed by each modality. It also holds out a substantive account of many perceptual deficits. For example, someone who is 'red/green' color blind, as this common deficit is relevantly but unperspicuously named, may be operating with a color phase space that has collapsed from a 3-D volume to a 2-D plane, because one of the normal axes is in him inoperative.

I must mention also that this 'phase-space position' account of perceptual representation is part of a larger account of brain function that embraces computations on these phase-space representations as well. The brain, it seems, embodies the machinery to perform coordinate transformations from one phase space to another. This allows us to account for a large class of computational activities, including those that sustain the sophisticated sensorimotor coordination displayed by cognitive creatures. The details of this highly general approach to brain function are outlined in my (1985b).

The account just sketched, of the qualitative character of sensations, suggests a useful vocabulary with which to describe individual qualia. Perhaps we shall be able to learn to specify, introspectively, and yet exactly, the 'ineffable' pink of one's visual sensation as a '95/70/70 hz spiking triplet,' and the smell of a new rose as a '23/4/15/88/60/12 hz olfactory chord' (cf. Churchland, 1985a). Such linguistic or conceptual replacement would not in this case amount to an ontological elimination, for we are supposing it to be motivated by a successful reduction. In the case of a reduction, linguistic reform is a luxury, though often a compelling one. In the case of an elimination, by contrast, linguistic reform becomes a necessity.

Sensations, I have argued, are reducible. More, no doubt, will also prove reducible. But much, we should be prepared for it, will be seriously revised or thrown out entirely. The latter is a prospect to be anticipated with especial intrigue, and we are well equipped to deal with it. For we *are* epistemic engines, and we *can* learn what once seemed impossible, so long as it is true.

Received March, 1985

References

P.M. Churchland, 'Two Grades of Evidential Bias,' *Philosophy of Science*, **42** (1975), 250-59

__________ *Scientific Realism and the Plasticity of Mind* (Cambridge: Cambridge University Press 1979)

____________ 'Eliminative Materialism and the Propositional Attitudes,' *Journal of Philosophy*, **78** (1981) 67-90

P.M. Churchland and P.S. Churchland, 'Functionalism, Qualia, and Intentionality,' *Philosophical Topics*, **12** (1981) 121-46. Reprinted in J. Biro and R. Shahan, eds., *Mind, Brain, and Function* (Normann, OK: University of Oklahoma Press 1982)

P.M. Churchland, 'The Anti-Realist Epistemology of Van Fraassen's *The Scientific Image*,' *Pacific Philosophical Quarterly*, **63** (1982) 226-36

____________, *Matter and Consciousness* (Cambridge, MA: MIT Press 1984)

____________, 'Reduction, Qualia, and the Direct Introspection of Brain States,' *Journal of Philosophy*, **82** (1985a), 8-28

____________, 'Cognitive Neurobiology: A Computational Basis for Laminar Cortex,' *Journal of Philosophy and Biology*, **1** (1985b)

Patricia S. Churchland, 'Consciousness: The Transmutation of a Concept,' *Pacific Philosophical Quarterly*, **64** (1983) 80-95

P.K. Feyerabend, 'How to be a Good Empiricist,' in B. Baumrin, ed., *Philosophy of Science, The Delaware Seminar*, Vol. 2 (New York, N.Y.: Interscience Publications 1963) 3-19. Reprinted in H. Morick, *Challenges to Empiricism* (Belmont, CA: Wadsworth 1972)

P.K. Feyerabend, 'Science Without Experience,' *Journal of Philosophy*, **66** (1969) 791-5

Edwin Land, 'The Retinex Theory of Color Vision,' *Scientific American*, December, 1977, 108-20

R. Nisbett and L. Ross, *Human Inference: Strategies and Shortcomings of Social Judgment* (New Jersey: Prentice Hall 1980)

R. Nisbett and T. Wilson, 'Telling More Than We Can Know: Verbal Reports on Mental Processes,' *Psychological Review*, **84** (1977) 231-59

CANADIAN JOURNAL OF PHILOSOPHY
Supplementary Volume 11

The Inward and the Outward: Fantasy, Reality and Satisfaction

CHRISTOPHER CHERRY
Eliot College
University of Kent at Canterbury
Canterbury, GB CT2 7NZ

I

Imagination works upon desires and needs in a variety of ways. Different sensibilities will concentrate upon different of its operations and neglect – or even ignore – others. Thus Rousseau (and in some ways Plato, as we shall see) takes a very gloomy view of the uses of imagination. He sees only its dark aspect, under which it is a prime source of wretchedness:

> It is imagination which enlarges the bounds of possibility for us ... and therefore stimulates and feeds desires by the hope of satisfying them. But the object within our grasp flies quicker than we follow; when we think we

> have grasped it, it transforms itself and is again ahead of us ... Thus we exhaust our strength, yet never reach our goal, and the nearer we are to pleasure, the further we are from happiness ... The world of reality has its bounds, the world of imagination is boundless; as we cannot enlarge the one, let us restrict the other; for all the sufferings which really make us miserable arise from the difference between the real and the imaginary.[1]

If we were forced to choose between Rousseau's perception and that expressed in adages like 'a man's reach should exceed his grasp' we ought, I am sure, to take the former as the less inadequate. Though partial, it is profound in ways the other is not. But perhaps we are not forced to make this choice even if, in the end, we find ourselves facing others which look rather like it. For if imagination makes us suffer by apprising or reminding us of what we haven't got and can't have, at the same time and by the same token it seems to go some way at least to removing or soothing the frustrations it itself induces. May it not on occasion be the disease of which it is if not the cure, at any rate the palliative? After all, one of the uses of imagination is precisely to cope with the miseries of deprivation: it is a banality that people 'take refuge in' imaginative flights of fancy, seek escape in day-dreams about being and doing what they cannot in reality be and do. And in such cases they are, presumably, not simply or primarily concentrating upon 'the *difference* between the real and the imaginary' but in some manner seeking to draw the two closer together by procuring within the imagination satisfactions unattainable outside. Here, it might be claimed, is a bright side to imagination which complements the dark side Rousseau focusses upon.

Now, there is some truth and much obscurity in the idea of imagination as therapy,[2] and certain varieties and implications of this

---

1 Excerpted from *Emile*, trans. B. Foxley (New York: Everyman's Library 1974), 44-5.

2 I am well aware that some psychotherapists swear by 'fantasy therapies,' but I have nothing so specific or technical (or suspect) in mind. And even if such therapies help in limited ways with, for instance, psychosexual problems it is worth remembering that remedies are also sought *for* excessive – and damaging – fantasising. Fantasts, it seems, are liable to horrors like Munchausen's Syndrome and Pseudologia Fantastica.

idea are the theme of my paper. I must say immediately that I am mainly concerned with one mode of the imagination, fantasy, and with that highly selectively, as it connects epistemologically and ethically with a person's desires and satisfactions.[3] In a moment, I want to identify and explore two sorts of connection. First, however, I shall show the power of Rousseau's dark view of the situation: that imagination creates, and where it does not create, intensifies wants and needs the frustrations of which it goes no way to relieve.

II

This is how things are to Maggie Tulliver:

> [E]very book in the world seemed so hard and unkind to Maggie: there was no indulgence, no fondness, such as she imagined when she fashioned the world afresh in her own thoughts. In books there were people who were always agreeable or tender, and delighted to do things that made one happy ... The world outside books was not a happy one. [Maggie] was a creature of eager, passionate longing for all that was beautiful and glad: thirsty for all knowledge: with an ear straining after dreamy music that died away and would not come to her: with a blind, unconscious yearning for something that would link together the wonderful impressions of this mysterious life and give her soul a sense of home in it.[4]

Maggie's imagination creates and progressively increases what Rousseau calls 'the difference between the real and the imaginary' and Eliot 'the contrast between the outward and the inward';[5] and yet it is

---

3 For fairly exhaustive treatments of fantasy by psychologists see J.L. Singer, *Daydreaming and Fantasy* (London: Allen and Unwin 1975), and K.J. Gilhooly, *Thinking: Directed, Undirected and Creative* (London: Academic Press 1982), ch. 6. Neither work appears even to recognise the existence of *philosophical* issues of the sort I pursue here.

4 George Eliot, *The Mill on the Floss* (Ontario: Penguin Books 1979), 319-20.

5 *Ibid.*, 320

powerless to mitigate the miseries produced by her reflection upon that difference, that contrast. Having induced and subsequently exacerbated the disease her reveries can provide no remedy. For Maggie as for Rousseau, imagination offers neither refuge nor escape: it is rather the opposite. We know pretty well what Maggie's needs are, and that they can be met only by massive changes in her external circumstances. They cannot, in Eliot's words, be met 'by means entirely within her own soul, without the help of outward things.'[6]

Now, the 'inward means' actually explored by Eliot and found wanting by Maggie are not, as might have been expected, those of the therapeutic imagination. It is not that Maggie tries, and fails, to gain some degree of solace from fashioning 'the world afresh in her own thoughts.' Perhaps, like Rousseau, Eliot didn't recognise that side of the imagination. More probably, she decided that it couldn't furnish an 'inward means' to *Maggie*, given the sort of person she was and the kind of needs she had. The means she explores, and on Maggie's behalf ultimately rejects, is a peculiarly self-destructive form of renunciation. 'With all the hurry of an imagination that could never rest in the present' Maggie sets about 'forming plans of self-humiliation and entire devotedness ... [R]enunciation seemed to her the entrance into that satisfaction which she had so long been craving in vain ... [H]ere was a sublime height to be reached without the help of outward things.'[7]

Although both may be accounted inward therapies, imaginative fantasy and renunciation are clearly means to very different mediate ends: the latter seeks to *eliminate* cravings like Maggie's by denying them long and hard enough, the former to *satisfy* them, after a fashion. Now, such is Hetty Sorel's fashion in her attempt to cope

---

6 *Ibid.*, 383

7 *Ibid.*, 383-4. The solution proposed, and promptly rejected, by Eliot to Maggie's problem of the 'contrast between the outward and the inward' is the one Rousseau stays with. Claiming that 'misery consists, not in the lack of things, but in the needs which they inspire' Rousseau exhorts us to minimize the difference between desires and powers (*Ibid.*, 45). Eliot, by contrast, has Maggie come to realise that 'renunciation remains sorrow, though a sorrow borne willingly' (*Ibid.*, 385).

with a hopeless passion for Captain Arthur Donnithorne. This is an excerpt from one of her extended fantasies:

> No eyelashes could be more beautiful than Hetty's, and now, while she walks with her pigeon-like stateliness along the room and looks down on her shoulders bordered by the old black lace, the dark fringe shows to perfection on her pink cheek. They are but dim, ill-defined pictures that her narrow bit of an imagination can make of the future; but of every picture she is the central figure, in fine clothes; Captain Donnithorne is very close to her, putting his arm round her, perhaps kissing her, and everybody else is admiring and envying her ...[8]

Maggie tried, without success, one kind of inward solution to the problem of desires unsatisfied. Hetty tries a different kind – in her case one which is imposed rather than self-consciously adopted. Her imagination brings her some measure of relief, however temporary and limited. Were her needs less urgent and overwhelming it would, we know, have brought more. So we have in Hetty's case, by contrast with Maggie's, an instance of imagination operating in a way discounted by Rousseau: it affords, in Eliot's words, an inward 'entrance into satisfaction' open, in differing degrees, to probably everyone. Thus it is that the inward can be made, *faute de mieux*, to substitute for the outward. An inner performance goes proxy for an external process or state of affairs in such a way that an object of desire – person, thing, accomplishment, life-style – is possessed in imagination *instead of* reality. I call this kind of fantasy performance, deputising as it does for the real thing, *surrogate fantasy*, and whatever degree of satisfaction derives from it *surrogate satisfaction*. I want in a moment to contrast it with fantasy of a different kind which does not substitute for anything more real and which yields a satisfaction which is not surrogate. This kind I shall call *autonomous fantasy*.

The ideas of surrogate-fantasy and surrogate satisfaction are complex and difficult to understand. This is so especially when substitute objects of desire are, as in the present instance, inner and private

---

8 George Eliot, *Adam Bede* (London: Collins 1952), 143. Chapter 15 is in effect a description of Hetty's recurrent fantasies about herself and Arthur Donnithorne – her inward solution given the lack of an outward.

rather than outward and public. I shall indicate some of these complexities when I contrast surrogate and autonomous fantasy. For immediate purposes I shall make three points about the former kind. First, it should not be thought that fantasising such as Hetty's is a single-minded and exclusive pursuit of surrogate-satisfaction. For one thing, activities of this kind are rarely that deliberate and controlled; for another, they are often (if not always) other things as well. In so far as Hetty half-believes that she will actually marry Arthur Donnithorne her fantasies are inner rehearsals of what she hopes will at some point become realities. So her satisfaction is at once surrogate and anticipatory.[9] In the second place – a point to which I shall return – it would be ridiculous to suppose that once delegated to the imagination surrogate-satisfaction is assured or lasting, or rich, or undilute, in anything like the way it might be if needs and wants were *actually* met. Even with Hetty, whose grip on reality is feeble, moments of 'chill daylight and reality come across her dream.'[10]

Thirdly, surrogate-fantasies do not necessarily, and perhaps even typically, represent what they are surrogates for in so coherent and mimetic a way as Hetty's does. They are often allusive and oblique, as Wittgenstein reminds us: 'If we hold it a truism that people take pleasure in imagination, we should remember that this imagination is not like a painted picture or a three-dimensional model, but a complicated structure of heterogeneous elements.'[11]

---

9 There need be no element of rehearsal, though. '[C]hronic prison daydreamers dreamed nearly always of the future – and of the past only as it might have been, never as it actually *had* been' (Arthur Koester, *Darkness at Noon* (Ontario: Penguin Books 1983), 45).

10 Eliot, *Adam Bede*, 224. Hetty, George Eliot tells us, is 'a woman spinning in young ignorance a light web of folly and vain hopes which may one day close round her and press upon her, a rancorous, poisoned garment changing all at once her fluttering, timid butterfly sensations into a life of deep human anguish' (*Ibid.*, 227).

11 'Remarks on Frazer's *Golden Bough*', *The Human World*, 3 (1971), 18-41

III

It is part of the logic of the subrogation that I make the best of a bad job. What I really (primarily) want is out of reach and its place is taken by a substitute. Whatever satisfaction ensues is strictly *faute de mieux*. In the case of fantasy we can express this in two conditions. First, primary want and object are external to and presupposed by their fantasy surrogate. Secondly, as an instrument for satisfying in some measure a primary want fantasy may be more or less effective. Thus, Hetty wants Arthur but can possess him only fleetingly and insubstantially in imagination. Maggie's is the limiting case – the case Rousseau took to be the only possible: she wants compassion, tenderness and fondness, but her imagination serves not to soothe but to intensify her wants. Her fantasies constitute no surrogate and yield no satisfaction.

Consider now a very different kind of case. Want and object are internal and not external to fantasy performance; they are created by it and have no life apart from it, no application to a world outside it. Fanatasy here is not a substitute, a make-do, for some more real fulfilment, for there just is no outward desideratum which the inward goes surrogate for. By contrast with surrogate fantasy, it is in the logic of this kind – autonomous fantasy – that imagination should bring *ultimate* satisfaction. The difference between the two kinds is captured in that between two senses to the claim that a desire can find satisfaction only in imagination. Taken in one way – the surrogate – it means that in the circumstances the best I can do is to fantasise. Taken in another – the autonomous – it means that fantasy alone makes possible the desire of which it is itself the complete satisfaction. It is not that imagination is, *faute de mieux*, the only way to satisfy the desire, but that it is the only way to *have* it.[12] Consider the following excerpt from an essay by Lynne Segal:

---

12 Analogously, why shouldn't the wishes which some people think are, on occasion, fulfilled in dreams be sometimes wishes only in dreams? Dreams would sometimes be the only way not merely to satisfy wishes but *to have them* in the first place. This would not, incidently, disallow dreams a role in the real world: a part of their purpose might still be to prepare us for *any* eventuality, including the worst. (As, indeed, Wittgenstein suggests in *Culture and Value* (Oxford: Blackwells 1979), 73.

> The fantasies which I have always needed ... are for me far more tedious and obnoxious. In them I am always passive, objectified, humiliated and whatever abuse I can imagine to be happening at the time also contains the threat of even worse to follow ... I resent the content of the fantasies. And I resent the effort I have to make to produce them, and the disconnection which occurs with lovers who, at least recently, are most caring, gentle, and as extensively physically stimulating as I would wish.[13]

And a little later she writes:

> The problem with masochistic fantasy, I find, is *not at all* that it encourages real submissiveness, and most certainly *not* any desire for real pain, hurt or humiliation ... I could feel, of course, that my masochistic fantasies provide me with an 'autonomous sexuality' – it is always me who is in control. But the problem is *I don't want to be*.[14]

Segal's avowals are complex and I shall later pursue certain issues they raise. For immediate purposes, however, they illustrate perfectly what I mean by autonomous fantasy: what Segal craves in fantasy she does not want in reality: the former is emphatically not a substitute for the latter, as it is for Hetty.

We have seen how Rousseau imputes most miseries to the difference between the real and the imaginary, intending by this the disequilibrium between our powers and our will: 'True happiness consists in decreasing the difference between our desires and our powers, in establishing a perfect equilibrium between the power and the will.'[15] His diagnosis is right for Maggie and half-right for Hetty – only half-right because in his concentration upon the disease caused by imagination he disregards the palliative it can bring. And yet, on the face of it, it is utterly wrong for Lynne Segal, seeming as it does to by-pass cases, like hers, of autonomous fantasy. For such cases are precisely those

---

13 Sue Cartledge and Joanne Ryan, eds., *Sensual Uncertainty in Sex and Love, New Thoughts on Old Contradictions* (London: The Women's Press Limited 1983), 42.

14 *Ibid.*, 42 (Italics in original)

15 *Ibid.*, 44

where there *is* no gap between power and will. To adapt a remark of Wittgenstein, they are cases where in representing a desire my imagination thereby not only portrays but *secures* its fulfilment.[16] Autonomous fantasy guarantees total satisfaction in the respect that my powers cannot fail to be the measure of my desires: in this dimension perfect equilibrium is assured just so long as there are no *technical* hitches – my reveries being inopportune, or interrupted, or my being distracted, and the like. (And even then one's inclination is to say that desire disappears rather than it is left unsatisfied.)

But there is another dimension in which autonomous fantasy may leave a person deeply and chronically unsatisfied: that in which he or she is *dissatisfied* with the difference between the real and the imaginary, in a sense other than that Rousseau had in mind and we have seen to apply, in varying degrees, to surrogate fantasy. In this other sense, the difference is not one between what is desired and what is possible but one between what is desired in imagination and what is desired in reality. The miseries which now come do not result from a failure to get what one wants (this is taken care of) but from an acknowledgement of *contradictory* wants. So the kind of dissatisfaction which is an inescapable feature of surrogate fantasy cannot likewise be one of autonomous fantasy, but by the same token, dissatisfaction with the contradiction between fantasy needs and the real needs – a dissatisfaction which supervenes upon autonomous fantasising – dissatisfaction of this kind cannot conceivably infect surrogate fantasy. A cynic might say that it is all a question of swings and roundabouts.

---

16 'Remarks on Frazer's *Golden Bough*', 31. Writing about fairy tales Freud aptly captures the world of autonomous fantasy, with its geography of 'wish-fulfilments, secret powers, omnipotence of thoughts.' The 'world of reality' is left behind from the very start 'by the postulates of the world of fairy tales,' and things regarded as incredible become possible. ('The Uncanny', trans. Alix Strachey, 250.) We need not of course follow Freud when he argues that primitive 'forms of thought which have become surmounted-animism, belief in magic and the omnipotence of thoughts' are in essence fantasies which, unlike fairy stories, refuse to leave the real world behind. The account more appropriately applies to pathological fantasts, who blur or ignore the boundary between fantasy and reality.

Now, I do not think that dissatisfaction with contradictory wants must be a feature of autonomous fantasy as dissatisfaction with what is unfulfilled must be a feature of surrogate fantasy. For one thing, there can be varying degrees of conflict and disharmony which stop short of opposition. And indeed, an autonomous fantast may want nothing in reality which can contradict what he or she wants in fantasy – not because the wants agree, for that would return us to surrogates, but because reality-directed counterparts to specific fantasy wants are quite simply lacking. Thus, instead of desiring real gentleness and care whilst contradictorily seeking fantasy humiliation and abuse Segal might have been *indifferent* to realities, with no desires one way or the other. (Of course, this might well occasion dissatisfaction of another sort.) For another thing, a person might clearly recognise very real contradictions *and yet not give a damn.* That this should so often be the case seems to me bad, and I shall return to it at the end.

The fact remains that Segal gives very much of a damn as her talk of 'tedious and obnoxious' fantasies, of 'resentment,' 'disconnection' and 'fragmentation,' testifies. She is distressed by the contradiction she acknowledges between what she demands from reality and what she demands (and gets) from imagination. The distress which comes from and feeds on reflection upon this sort of difference between the real and the imaginary is in both quality and depth quite different from the distress which derives from recognition of the difference between power and will, the sort of difference between the real and the imaginary that surrogate-fantasy seeks to bridge. It is the sort of distress Plato thinks we ought to experience when, speaking of poetry and drama rather than of self-inspired fantasy, he writes:

> [We] admire, when we see him on stage, a man we should ourselves be ashamed to resemble. Is it reasonable to feel enjoyment and admiration rather than disgust?[17]
>
> [You] enjoy on the stage – or even in ordinary life – jokes you would be ashamed to make yourself, instead of detesting their vulgarity.[18]

17 Plato, *The Republic* (Ontario: Penguin Books 1974), 436

18 *Ibid.*, 437. Cf. Wittgenstein, *Culture and Value*, 87: God may say to me: 'I am judging you out of your own mouth, your own actions have made you shudder with disgust when you have seen other people do them.'

Plato thought such contradictions so 'unreasonable' that what nourished them should, as far as possible, be removed. Might not the same be said of the contradictions in ourselves which Segal notes, for they are after all just a special – and especially acute - case? I shall take up this question in my conclusion; but first I have more to say about the relationship between subrogation and autonomy.

IV

Earlier I distinguished surrogate from autonomous fantasy by arguing that whereas in the former case a desired object is external to and presupposed by fantasising which can be more or less – usually less – effective in providing substitute satisfaction, in the latter case an object is desired only within fantasy and therefore cannot in any substantial sense remain unsatisfied. To this may be added the further contrast just examined: the dissatisfaction characteristically accompanying surrogate fantasy is dissatisfaction with the gap that remains, despite the fantasy therapy, between power and will, reality and desire. By contrast, the dissatisfaction which often comes from autonomous fantasising is one with a different opposition: the opposition between what is desired in reality and what is desired in imagination.

How shall we know if a fantasy is surrogate or autonomous? At its simplest, our appeal must be to that modern Polycrates, Jimmy Savile: how will a fantasiser react to the promise (or as it may seem, threat) that the real thing can be arranged? Will he or she jump at the chance, or run a mile? Now, while it is immediately obvious what Hetty Sorel or Lynne Segal would do if Jim promised to fix it, many cases are nothing like so accommodating as theirs. This fact, suitably developed, might be thought to imperil the distinction by suggesting, in particular, two kinds of objection to any Jim'll-fix-it test, no matter how refined. The first is that when set the test many people will have no idea what to say. The second is that the tester has no very good reason for taking what they do say seriously anyway. I shall try and deal with these objections in turn.

The first, that people will often not know how to respond, is not in fact a problem for the distinction itself – although if true it is disappointing. It is not a problem since the thesis that there are (at least) two importantly different kinds of fantasy does not require there will be, or could be, or even must be in respect of any and every fantasy a hard-and-fast answer to the question: surrogate or autonomous? That is, it does not demand that every fantasy should be *absolutely* of the one kind or the other, let alone that subjects will always be able to classify their performances. No one supposes, for instance, that the distinction between identity and similarity is threatened, just because there are tiresomely familiar cases where it is a matter of indifference whether we speak of sameness or similarity, since neither description is any more or less acceptable than the other. It is sufficient that the distinction between surrogate and autonomous applies at least commonly, albeit not usually with the sharpness characteristic of Hetty's and Lynne Segal's cases.

But although properly understood it is no objection to the distinction, the claim that people will often be unable to answer the Jim'll-fix-it test cover different sorts of case and I shall mention one or two. First of all, there are cases where refinements to the test are likely to produce answers. Then there are cases where people remain in two minds about whether they really want to do or be or have what they imagine doing or being or having. (Their uncertainty may show itself in their sometimes responding positively and sometimes negatively.) Some, but probably not most, autoerotic fantasies are of this sort. The bittersweet jokes people make about them ('You meet a better class of person that way,' 'At least it's sex with someone you love,' 'Sex with someone is great but it's nothing like the real thing') suggest an uneasy oscillation between surrogate and autonomous fantasising which is not adequately accounted for in terms of mood and fantasy-content. This is confirmed by a recent literature which has, in deadly earnest, provided firm sexual-political grounds for the uncertainties.[19]

---

19 Thus, one (but only one) reason why a person may be reluctant to categorise autoerotic fantasies is an uncertainty about what ought to be said, about what saying one thing rather than another commits one to. Until fairly recently it has been taken for granted by almost all writers on the subject that rational,

In the third place, there is an extensive category of cases where uncertainties about whether or not fantasised desires spill over into the real world derive from initial indeterminacies about what is desired. Some desires have obscure objects, and in such cases it is difficult, not to say impossible, to know what would and would not count as satisfying them in the real world. What, exactly, would the actualization of certain fantasises be like? And here I am thinking not just, or even mainly, of fantasies, like the Gygean, with impossible objects – distinction and test alike cut across the possible-impossible axis and it would not be ridiculous to say that the best thing to do with the impossible is to fantasise it – but of sustained fantasy performances like the following:

> It's 12.15 am. The nightclub is already packed. He makes his entrance, a vision in black and gold – black silk shirt unbuttoned almost to the waist, black trousers, black shoes, and gold everywhere. Three gold medallions dangling on his chest, two gold rings on the same hand. He's about forty, his hair cropped short, he's smoking a cigar. He walks slowly in a cool, rather confident manner, scanning the faces. He greets the bouncers, they greet him. Don Corleone is back ... But Don Corleone is not what he seems. He's an Italian waiter from a restaurant in a Northern industrial town. He hasn't any money, he hasn't even got a car ... When he's standing at the bus stop during the day, with a bag of washing for the laundrette, he positively jumps into hiding if he spots anybody he recognises. He lives alone in a bedsitter. Luigi, the waiter, by day – Don Corleone, the somebody, by night.[20]

---

non-pathological desire is for sex with a partner, masturbatory fantasising its surrogate, performed for want of anything better. Masturbation because nothing *is* better was rarely noted as an option – and, when it was, despised and condemned (Sartre calls it 'dishonest,' Laing 'evasive'). But it has become increasingly clear that for some people sometimes, if not always, fantasised sex with themselves is the preferred and not a substitute mode: binary sex, with the intrusive presence of another, is either nowhere, or repugnant. See, for instance, Angela Phillips and Jill Rakusen, eds., *Our Bodies Ourselves* (Ontario: Penguin Books 1978), ch. 3; and Alan Soble, ed., *Philosophy of Sex* (Totowa, NJ: Rowman and Littlefield 1980), passim, and especially Jacqueline Fortunata, 'Masturbation and Women's Sexuality.'

20 From a recent piece to entertain readers of the 'Guardian' newspaper about 'some extra-ordinary men who lead extraordinary double lives.'

What does Luigi's fantasy substitute for? Being Don Corleone? Being some mafia Godfather or other in the mould of Don Corleone? Being a powerful and ruthless exhibitionist? It is unclear, probably to Luigi and certainly to everyone else, just how the world would have to rearrange itself to meet his needs. It is however clear that his fantasising will seem able to accommodate some specifications less incompletely than others – to the point, indeed, that under certain descriptions his wants will appear to be completely met within the confines of imagination: fantasy will come to seem all that Luigi needs. To generalise: where desires are indeterminate or obscure, the kind, if any, to which a fantasy is allocated will be a function of determinations which are at the very least hazardous. Now this, if correct, has implications which I can only note here. Fantasies which are as consistent, regular, time-consuming and elaborate as Luigi's seem in the end to take all force away from the contrast between fantasy and reality (and hence from its sub-contrasts). And we might do better in such cases to talk instead of contrasting *realities*.[21] But rather than develop the two faces of Luigi, I want to make two less speculative points. First, fantasies like Luigi's do not represent real possibilities – possible realities – with anything like the fidelity common to Hetty's and Segal's. This is one reason why they leave so much room for interpretation. (One is inclined to say: 'The more faithful the fantasy the less satisfying it is.') Secondly, although themselves the protagonists, the Luigis of this world would on the face of it seem no better, and arguably rather worse, placed than some others to make whatever fantasy-interpretations (desire-determinations) are called for.

This brings me to the second line of objection to the Jim'll-fix-it test, that there can be no good reason to take a fantasiser's answers seriously. In most of its forms it is no more successful than the first

21 To develop this would demand exploring far more single-mindedly the idea of subrogation. How, for example, are we to construe claims like: Proust treated writing, and Plato treated virtue 'as a continuation of life by other means'? I discuss some of these issues in 'Can my Survival be Subrogated?', *Philosophy*, 59 (1984) 443-56. See also my 'Games and the World,' *Philosophy*, 51 (1976) 57-61.

and, like it, establishes at most that the surrogate-autonomous distinction does not apply universally to fantasy.

Thus, we scarcely need telling that people can lie, be self-deceived and give wrong answers because they are confused about grounds: for instance, a person might insist that no, he wouldn't want to really do or be what he imagines himself doing or being and yet back this with grounds – timidity, sluggishness, anxieties – which in fact explain why he takes no steps to actualise his wants and instead delegates them to fantasy. There is, however, one form in which the objection does threaten the distinction, and I must deal with it.

Lynne Segal, it will be remembered, only *has* certain needs when fantasising: she emphasises that the last thing she desires is 'real pain, hurt or humiliation.' Her fantasies are paradigmatically autonomous. Suppose it were now objected that 'a part of her' (or whatever) certainly *does* want real pain, hurt and humiliation and hence that her wants are not, after all, internal to the play of imagination but spill over into the real world. Her fantasies are in fact surrogates, though complex and murky ones. Now, this line can of course be taken with every candidate autonomous fantasy, reducing it more or less swiftly to one of the surrogate variety, so let me outline how I think the reduction can and must be resisted. The very considerations which incline some to insist, despite the agent's sincere denial, that what she or he wants to do or be in imagination is necessarily a more or less faithful representation of and substitute for what she or he wants in actuality – these considerations may equally well be construed as *explanations* why autonomous fantasy should create and satisfy wants taking this or that form and direction. Segal in fact mentions some such considerations:

> Sexism and repressive attitudes to sex have certainly fed these (masochistic) fantasies. But on a more personal level I think they began as consolations for particular circumstances of a quite extreme experience of loneliness in infancy and childhood, with the magical belief that somehow reparation should and would be made for suffering. I see them as, among other things, a way of making myself the centre of attention, when in fact I knew for certain that there was actually nobody there for me at all in reality.[22]

22 Segal, 45

One may or may not accept Segal's interpretation. My point is that if one does, one is not thereby forced – or even encouraged, so far as I can see – to construe her fantasies as substitutes for some more real thing: actual masochistic reparation. Rather, one is better equipped to understand why precisely these wants and needs seek and find satisfaction. Certainly they appear to have *causal antecedents* in the real world. But this is very different from insisting, in the face of contrary protestations, that they are *addressed to* realities and that their ultimate satisfaction demands outward expression. And the converse holds: desires directed towards bringing about changes in the real world may for all that have originated within the imagination and subsequently come to lead a life of their own, away from the inward processes which gave birth to them. Maggie Tulliver's wants, we are told, derived from reflections upon books she read and yet once made her own were precisely not satisfiable *within* those reflections.

If this is less than wholly convincing it is, I hope, because so much more needs to be said, and in particular about what traffic there might be between surrogate and autonomous fantasy. However that may be, even if autonomous fantasy were in the end to collapse into surrogate, it would be at a depth which leaves undisturbed many levels of important difference. I shall conclude with some remarks about one such level, the ethical.

V

In laid back frames of mind we allow ourselves an indulgent overview of the imagination as fantast and daydreamer. So occupied, it is variously smug, foolish, shameless, contempible, ruinous – and also vital and delicious. It's a funny old world, we reflect. But our mood can be different: even within the narrow (and idealized) area I have been considering we find occasion to condemn – and sometimes even applaud. Our grounds are mixed, of course; but all in all they tend to suggest something like the following radically incomplete moral epistemology.

Because they are at one remove or more from reality the products of fantasy can be evil or good only at one remove or more. Parasites, they must derive whatever moral significance they possess from an association with realities. But what sort of association? Well, in order for imaginary doing or being X to be *itself* evil or good it cannot be sufficient, although it must be necessary, that actually doing or being X is evil or good. For were it sufficient, the required association between imagination and reality would be one merely of ideas, and the ascription of moral quality to the former nothing but a bad case of unreasoned analogy. What is further required is that the imagination should be seen to be somehow actively, albeit indirectly, *implicated* in actual evil – and good – doing. To this end, fantasising is taken as a matter of course to be criterial of desires to act on and in the real world, and as such a surrogate for real activity: I would if I could but right now I can't ... The association between imagination and reality has now been made intentional, but at least two further – quasi-empirical – claims are commonly added (and with good reason: for how a fantasised *substitute* for actual evil or good thereby becomes itself evil or good is wholly obscure). The first is that fantasising reinforces desires to act: the more a person imagines doing A the more entrenched and powerful becomes his need to A, and the more likely it is to actualize itself when opportunity presents. The second is that fantasy, and above all commercial fantasy, originates desires and needs which because they become reality-directed, it cannot itself satisfy. This, it will be recalled, was the case with Maggie Tulliver.

My quarrel is not – or rather, is not here – with the truth or detailed logic of these claims, however suspect. It is with a central implication of the over-reaching moral epistemology which grounds them and which they in turn shore up: it writes off autonomous fantasy – and no doubt much else also – as a serious subject for ethics. For it connects *all* fantasy-creations with reality in such a way that they can possess moral significance only as its surrogates, necessarily wanting and constantly seeking the real thing. Now, this is unlikely to disturb those who will not acknowledge autonomous fantasy (although it should be noticed that by the same token they can never allow *intrinsic* value or disvalue to the surrogate variety). Nor will it bother those who recognise its existence but suppose that of its very nature it must be morally indifferent, *no matter what its content.* Those, however, who are all too well aware of it *and* believe (perhaps without knowing quite why) that it need not be morally neutral will have to look elsewhere for grounds. I shall end by suggesting, but no more, where they might start.

It seems to me that there are two starting-points which at first sight look very different. Both involve pursuing certain oppositions between imaginative fantasy and reality, but whereas the first path will lead us to a contrast between the illusory and the real (or at any rate the more real) the second will lead us to one between different realities. I shall take them in turn.

A moment ago I said, rather vaguely, that fantasy stands at one or more removes from reality. The vagueness was deliberate; for by definition surrogate fantasy is at least linked to reality as autonomous is not, and so is less far removed. (We need be no more precise: quantifying removes is a fairly arbitrary business, as anyone familiar with Plato's theory of art will know!) Now, it is well known that Plato argues that image-making of whatever kind is bad in proportion as its creations are removed from reality – from truth. Thus, he says many harsh things about the arts of representation: they trade in the 'second hand,' the 'unreal,' the 'artificial,' the 'apparent,' and as such are calculated to appeal to the 'ignorant and unreasoning' part of ourselves.[23] I am sure we should not dream of following Plato all, or even most, of the way, for there lies madness. But perhaps we can go thus far with him: autonomous fantasising is characteristically the production of images which are not merely not-real but *counter real*. They are not substitutes for but contradictions of realities, of real wants and needs. Now, glossing Plato, may we not say that the 'part of the mind which contradicts is an inferior one ... far removed from the truth and associated with elements in us equally far removed from reason, in a fond liaison without health or truth'?[24]

If we say this then we say it is bad. But we seem at one and the same time to say too much and too little. For what is bad is all autonomous fantasising, no matter how apparently benign the content; yet it is bad only for the fantasiser, – for, in Plato's words, 'the constitution of his inner self.' And, furthermore, why should it be bad for him

23 Plato, Bk. 10, passim

24 *Ibid.*, 432-3

if he just doesn't care about contradictions in himself? I cannot here hope to answer that question. But it may be possible to deal with the first two difficulties by taking the other route to moralising autonomous fantasy.

Throughout I have contrasted fantasy with reality. For many purposes this is perfectly acceptable – and indeed necessary. However, there is an equally acceptable although much broader sense of 'reality' in which fantasy is just one constituent of reality. It is that sense in which the images of our imagination are, no less than anything else, a part of the world we live in, experience and operate upon. Given this more encompassing concept of reality we can perfectly properly say that imagining doing something terrible to someone is, though very different from, no less (and no more) real than actually doing something terrible to her. And we can, if rather less confidently, add that the harm caused her by the imagined doing is very different from but no less a harm than that caused by the actual deed. No doubt *she* would have strong views about relative damages; yet even so, she might believe she was harmed – in respect, say, of her integrity and autonomy – by another's thinking about her in certain ways. Certainly actual physical violation might be perceived as a worse harm, but nonetheless as a separate and additional one. And perhaps something of this sort goes, *mutatis mutandis*, for benevolent and altruistic fantasies, too.

Of course, many people will think this idea of 'inward' harm a complete nonsense unless and until it is linked, however indirectly, to the familiar one of actual 'outward' damage. Likewise, they will suppose that when he censures us for laughing at stage jokes we would be ashamed to make ourselves Plato must either be alerting us to the dangers of becoming public buffoons or else talking rubbish; and again, that Lynne Segal's distress at inner self-contradiction is a neurotic self-indulgence. If they have a point, I suspect it is one that cannot be held to consistently. After all, everyone wants and needs to be well-thought of – even, if Aristotle is right, the dead.

Received September, 1984

CANADIAN JOURNAL OF PHILOSOPHY
Supplementary Volume 11

Amnesia and Psychological Continuity

ANDREW BRENNAN
University of Stirling
Stirling, Scotland FK9 4LA

I. The Problem

Is amnesia the mother of discontinuity? Perhaps surprisingly, amnesia is perfectly compatible with psychological continuity. Think, for example, of David Wiggins' version of Locke. Wiggins first describes a relation *C* of strong *co-consciousness* which gives continuity 'between person P_{tj} and person Q_{tk} such that, for some *sufficiency* of things actually done, witnessed, experienced, ... at any time by P_{tj}, Q_{tk} should later have *sufficient* real or apparent recollection of then doing, witnessing, experiencing, ... them.' Wiggins continues:[1]

1 'Locke, Butler and the Stream of Consciousness,' in A.O. Rorty, ed.: *The Identities of Persons* (Los Angeles: University of California Press 1976), 144.

> ... anyone bent on grasping the nerve of Locke's conception of person would see ... that the identity-condition he had to refute was one which made the persistence of person *P* depend only upon *P*'s being related at each successive phase of his biography in this C-relation to *P* at each previous phase

Clearly, strong co-consciousness is unlikely to be transitive; but the ancestral of this relation, *co-consciousness*, seems to provide a neo-Lockean identity condition: *A* is the same person as *B* iff *A* is co-conscious with *B*.

Now, provided we restrict P_{tj}'s access to past witnessings to those occurring only in the very recent past, and keep the temporal gap between P_{tj} and Q_{tk} likewise small, then an individual with intact short term memory but with little, or no, long term memory could display strong co-consciousness from one moment to the next. A day in the life of such an amnesic could be compared to a chalk being drawn across a blackboard with a duster an inch behind erasing all but the resulting line's immediate past. Temporal lobe amnesics are in precisely this situation; although they have intact cognitive abilities, including capacity for acquiring and retaining some motor skills, they lack long term memory, and so someone met in the morning would be greeted as a stranger in the afternoon.[2] Strong co-consciousness from moment to moment is thus, on its own, hardly a secure foundation from which to build up the psychological unity of self typical of the undamaged person.

We can contrast the psychologically continous experience of the temporal lobe amnesic with the psychological discontinuities of everyday life. Whatever consciousness is, we all seem to experience it as an episodic phenomenon whose discrete manifestations are interrupted by sleep, daydreams, absorption in certain sorts of task, and so on. It is unfortunate, indeed, that writers so often use the term *continuity* for what are clear cases of discontinuity. Thus consider some recent remarks of Derek Parfit's:[3]

---

2 See S.D. Iversen, 'Temporal Lobe Amnesia', in C.M. Whitty and O.L. Zangwill (eds): *Amnesia*, 2nd edition (London: Butterworths 1977).

3 Derek Parfit, 'Personal Identity and Rationality,' *Synthese* 53 (1982), 229.

> Suppose that I am about to die. Some future person who will not be *me*, will be fully continous with me ... He will thus take up my life where I left off, finishing my masterpiece, and caring for my children

Continuity here, so far from requiring co-consciousness from moment to moment, involves rather the notion that the next episode, no matter how far removed in time from the preceding one, goes on more or less where that preceding one left off. So that we do not confuse this notion with that of continuity conceived as a temporally continous succession of episodes (a sequence without gaps), I will for the moment use the term *coherence* to label the phenomenon Parfit describes. Whereas the amnesic might, in the course of a waking day, display psychological continuity but with no coherence between episodes remote in time, someone else may experience episodes of consciousness that are discontinous and remote in time from each other and yet cohere in an orderly way.

Since persons have bodies, one way of associating all the amnesic's psychological episodes with one person is by appeal to continuity of body. Likewise, a sequence of coherent, but discontinuous episodes become episodes in the life of one person if we are able to associate all of them with one continous body. If psychological (and emotional) states are software of a sort, and bodies are hardware, then the body criterion of personal identity is one way of grounding the identity of discrete bits of software in one concrete thing for which we think we have clear and unambiguous identity conditions. In this paper, I will not discuss the merits and drawbacks of bodily continuity as a criterion for personal identity, although it is worth remembering that this criterion seems to underlie our description of, and behaviour towards, amnesics and others whose psychological capacities are disordered or fragmented.

Suppose, though, for the sake of the argument, and in keeping both with some current conceptions of persons as software and with Locke's conception, we resist an appeal to any body criterion. Can we

---

Alas, I too have been careless in using the terminology of psychological continuity: see my 'Personal Identity and Personal Survival', *Analysis* **41** (1982) 44-50.

give a suitably detailed account of coherence which would explain what it is that makes a sequence of psychological episodes all episodes belonging to the same person?

II. Theories

In response to this last question, Parfit has suggested that such coherence is the result of overlapping chains of psychological *connectedness*. One's psychological state at one time is connected with one's state at another when the states are linked by memory, intention, and the like, or both manifest some enduring characteristic.[4] Again, as we found with co-consciousness, the temporal lobe amnesic will show connectedness over suitably brief intervals. The difference between Parfit's and Wiggins' notions is that the former is meant to admit of degrees. As far as speculation about our future or past is concerned, Parfit holds that *what matters* is survival, not identity. Suppose we take two psychological time-slices from the history of what seems to be one person. We can ask, now, to what extent one such earlier slice is connected, and 'continuous,' with a later slice. Suppose, for one case, that there are very rich connections running between the slices: memories in abundance, intentions carried out, ambitions, desires and other characteristics relatively stable, and so on. Mediating the two episodes are, we will imagine, even denser networks of connection from each to various intermediate episodes. Here we could say that the one slice is very highly connected with the other. In this case, Parfit would hold that the person at the earlier time survives, from a psychological point of view at least, in – or as – the person at the later time.

As we increase the temporal gap between the slices, the situation is likely to change. Even though the density of interconnections between successive and only slightly distanced, episodes stays constant, later slices tend to lose more and more of their direct connectedness with a

4 See his 'Personal Identity,' *Philosophical Review* **80** (1971) 3-27.

given earlier one. Thus memories fade, intentions and ambitions get forgotten, and even what once seemed basic, and stable characteristics start to change. But so long as at least some connectedness remains between a later and an earlier episode, then our person, in Parfit's view, can be said to survive to some degree. So we have here a means of talking about personal survival when the degree of communication between the slices is far less than the sufficiency that Wiggins is likely to require for co-consciousness to be present.

Thinking, in this way, of psychological episodes, or states, being connected or in communication with each other we can put the following question: how much intercommunication is required to work distinct episodes into the weave of a single life? In this connection, think of David Lewis's remarks:[5]

> ... what I mostly want in wanting survival is that my mental life should flow on. My present experiences, thoughts, beliefs, desires and traits of character should have appropriate future successors ... Change should be gradual rather than sudden, and (at least in some respects) there should not be too much change overall ... Such change as there is should conform, for the most part, to lawful regularities concerning the succession of mental states ...

The account I am about to give is meant to sketch a way of capturing what is correct in the co-consciousness and connectedness stories while giving us the means to discuss degrees of coherence. It will also capture, indeed explain, Lewis's insight that successions of mental episodes are lawfully ordered, while divorcing this from his commitment to continuity rather than coherence.

We can approach the question of the survival of one thing in, or as, another independently of the status of the things in question. At least, it seems worth *trying* to do this until we hit an obstacle that might convince us that at the level of the intentional, say, quite different considerations are involved from those operating at other levels. In an earlier paper, I worked out some of the details for a general account of survival, and I now want to suggest an elaboration

---

5 'Survival and Identity,' in A.O. Rorty, *The Identities of Persons*

of that account which can be applied, in the first instance, to concrete things.[6] As I will argue later, the *kind* of survival I am about to describe is not quite what Parfit has in mind, although it is related to the issue of survival as understood by him.

For the moment, let us suppose that a number of discrete, spatio-temporally discontinuous objects, are to be assigned to one, broader concrete object. The latter would be an *episodic* object with discontinous stages. Three conditions determine, in my view, the allocation of the stages to one thing: (i) the *matter* of each stage must be sufficiently similar to that of its successor; (ii) the *structure* of each stage must be likewise sufficiently similar to that of its successor; and (iii) that a successive stage has a certain matter and structure is *causally* dependent in an appropriate way on its immediate predecessor's having certain matter in a certain structure. Satisfaction of the three conditions justifies the claim that each stage *survives* as its successor and such a chain of survival relations can justify, I suggest, the allocation of the several stages to the one object.[7]

At the level of functional description suggested by the use of terms like *intention, need, desire, memory* and so on, a psychological state is not to be taken as a concrete item. Nevertheless, it is possible to look for analogues – metaphorical if you like – for the three conditions. The contents of short and long term memory, material undergoing perceptual processing, one's store of ambitions, intentions and so on can all be regarded as in some sense psychological *matter*. This

---

6 See 'Survival,' *Synthese* 59 (1984) 339-61.

7 I hope the conditions, despite the concise form of their introduction here, have a certain obviousness. I give a more detailed account of episodic objects, and of how the conditions work, in my paper 'Discontinuity and Identity.' (forthcoming in *Nous*) However, the conditions first occurred to me by considering the psychological cases: I regard their success in dealing with concrete objects as a confirmation of their general plausibility. In terms of the relative importance of the conditions, I argue in the *Synthese* paper mentioned in note 6 that structure is more significant than matter: it is perfectly intelligible to suppose that an item can survive a change in matter, so long as certain invariances of overall geometrical structure are preserved. The same is not true in the case where we change the structure and merely preserve an item's original matter.

material is no doubt *structured* within devices (thus long term memory has, among others, a semantic level of organisation) which themselves have *structural* relations with each other.[8] The recollecting from long term memory of an experience entered some time before would be an example of how a structural change in one state is in part *causally* dependent on a material (and associated structural) change in an earlier state.

Let us suppose – somewhat contentiously – that we have no experiences when asleep.[9] Then we can consider how the three conditions fare when applied to the relationship between my total psychological state this morning and my state as I fell asleep last night. There may well be changes, but these are outweighed by the manifold connections of structure and matter mediated by causal relations between the separated episodes. Think. to take a small example, of the poem I had been labouring to commit to mind yesterday evening: I rehearsed it haltingly as I was falling asleep, and this morning it comes to mind as I wake up. Here we have a strikingly clear case of the operation of our three conditions: the structure and material of my waking psychological state is causally connected in an appropriate way with that of the episode occurring as I fell asleep some hours before.

Although I have suggested that consciousness is episodic, I have refrained from claiming that our psychological life as a whole is discontinuous. Luckily, it is not necessary to pronounce on the question of whether this is so or not. For if we are unsure whether a series of episodes really is, or is not, continous in time we can still apply our three conditions to ascertain whether successive pairs of episodes cohere in the defined way. Of course, strong co-consciousness can only link psychological states that are states of consciousness. It may be that to be a *person* not only must some of an organism's psychological states be conscious states but that those states must have a certain

8 For a conjectured example of a small part of such a structure see the diagram in Daniel Dennett's *Brainstorms* (Sussex: Harvester Press 1978), 155.

9 Dennett writes: 'It is an *open* and *theoretical* question whether dreams fall inside or outside the boundary of experience,' *Brainstorms*, 147.

degree of coherence and connectedness with other *conscious* episodes. This kind of high-level view of the person would be very Lockean. But another possibility is that, to be one person, there should be manifestations of consciousness together simply with a more general psychological coherence. It is this second, somewhat weaker, view that I will characterise now.

Incidentally, the weaker notion of personhood seems to me much more plausible than the stronger one. A great deal of processing takes place without the subject's conscious awareness. Yet a person's styles of response to a range of situations will be strongly determined by just such hidden activity. What makes a friend a unique, distinctive, lovable, irritating, interesting person is not purely determined by what goes on at the level of conscious states. In this way *coherence*, as I use the notion, is wider than connectedness, or co-consciousness. For there may well be a high degree of coherence between distinct psychological episodes or states even in the presence of a low degree of connectedness in the form of memories, intentions and other elements present to consciousness. As we will see, the three conditions offer a way of dealing with just the kind of case that has been taken by some to provide a critical problem for the Lockean (see, for example, the discussion of amnesia in § VII of the Wiggins essay mentioned earlier).

III. Amnesia and the Branch-Line Case

Suppose that *a*, *b* and *c* in Figure 1 are extended phases of what commonsense (armed with a criterion of bodily continuity) would regard as one person, Pamela. During her *b*-phase, Pamela contracted – let us imagine – a serious intracranial infection which, for most of the time, did not affect her lucidity and which was successfully cured by t_2. Its legacy, however, was both an amnesia after t_2 with respect to events experienced during the illness itself together with a dense retrograde amnesia extending back from the onset of the illness to time t_1.

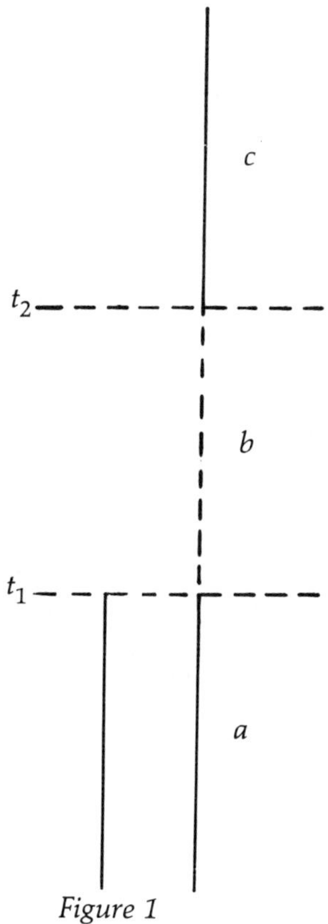

Figure 1

Althogh the *a*-phase is coherent with the *b*-phase (for even during her brief periods of delirium after the onset of the illness, Pamela revealed memories of the *a*-phase) it might seem that her *b*-phase does not cohere with her *c*-phase. In terms of Parfit's notion of *survival*, *a* survives as *b* and *a* survives as *c*, but some question seems to hang over whether *b* survives as *c*.

The temptation for the co-consciousness theorist is to admit that from t_2 onwards, Pamela's life is lived as if the *b*-phase had never occurred: *b* only survives as *c* to the extent that we can trace the *b*-phase *back* to the *a*-phase which itself runs on coherently to the *c*-phase. Thus Robert Elliot (again using the peculiar notion of continuity) writes of just this sort of case:[10]

> (take) three slices of the one person, P1, P2 and P3. P1 is standardly, psychologically continuous with P3 and P2. P2 and P3 are not standardly, psychologically continuous. However, since P2 and P3 are both standardly, psychologically continuous with P1, we can regard them as indirectly, psychologically continuous with each other.

Such 'indirect' coherence threatens to assimilate amnesia to the quite different case of fission or *branching*. For suppose that instead of an infection, the unfortunate Pamela had a problem that required the removal of half her brain. Before surgery, a special treatment allows both hemispheres to be brought into the same informational state, and, luckily, a donor body becomes available so that her right hemisphere – the one to be removed – can be transplanted. After surgery, her original body and left hemisphere linger for some time before being overtaken by death. The right hemisphere flourishes in its new body and that combination goes on to live for some considerable time. Since bodily continuity is not our concern, the psychological relations can be depicted as in Figure 2. Here the *b*-phase is the psychological history of the left hemisphere; both its

---

10 'Going Nowhere Fast?', *Analysis* 42 (1982), 214.

history, and the history of the right hemisphere associated with the *c*-phase, are taken to be discontinuous with the *a*-phase (on the, probably doubtful, assumption that a general anaesthetic destroys continuity of psychology).

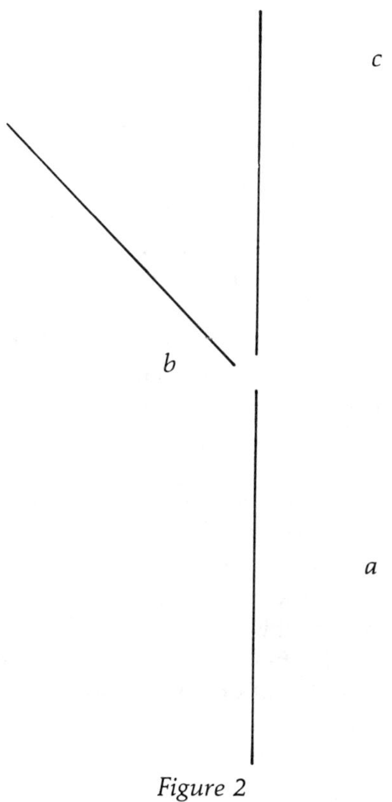

Figure 2

Derek Parfit has argued that amnesia shows some features in common with branching. For if our response to the Figure 2 situation is to admit that the *a*-phase does survive as the *c*-phase, we can again trace the *b*-phase back to the *a*-phase and claim that *it* is thus *indirectly* continuous (Parfit and Elliot) or coherent (me) with the *c*-phase. Oddly, then, the branching *b*-phase can survive as the *c*-phase. In terms of Parfit's useful metaphor, think of Pamela's *main-line* running from *a* to *c*, and *b* as a *branch-line*.[11] Both Parfit (explicitly) and Elliot (by implication) regard amnesia as a sort of *branch-line case*. One virtue of the account I am suggesting is that it allows us to separate at least some kinds of amnesia from the branching case.

Consider why the *c*-phase in both situations displays no memories of the *b*-phase. In the amnesia case, the causal account of this failure must make reference to Pamela's psychological states during the *b*-phase. These states were of course induced by the infection, itself not a psychological cause, but the mother of psychological effects. For simplicity, let us characterise some of the information reaching Pamela's psychological devices as subject to *consolidation*, *encoding* and subsequent *retrieval* in the normal course of events. One effect of the infection, let us suppose, was to render her encoding mechanisms non-operational, or seriously defective, for a time; so although she was behaving relatively normally, she was not processing any of her input in a way that would permit its subsequent retrieval.[12] Not only does this encoding defect explain why the *b*-phase did not show the normal structural changes associated with the entry of material into the long term store, but the absence of these changes also explains the subsequent absence of material and structure in the *c*-phase.

By contrast, the causal explanation of why, in the branching case, the *c*-phase has no memories of the *b*-phase involves no general dependence of the psychological matter and structure of the former on

---

11 The argument and terminology are from Derek Parfit's book, *Reasons and Persons* (Oxford: Oxford University Press 1984). I am grateful to him for the opportunity to read part of the book while it was still in draft form.

12 See M.F. Piercy, 'Experimental Studies of the Organic Amnesic Syndrome' in Whitty and Zangwill.

that of the latter. We can, of course, imagine building in microtransmitters and receivers that would provide an informational link between the two separated centres of consciousness. Then amnesia might be likened to certain kinds of failures in these electronic devices. But such a fantasy hardly represents the 'usual' branching case: for the intimacy of the link between the two hemispheres established by the addition of the gadgets gives us a case rather like that of one person with two bodies.[13]

The result is not unwelcome. It matches our natural tendency to count an illness that induces amnesia as an important episode in someone's life, explaining and contributing (albeit negatively) to subsequent episodes, while we would be reluctant to count branching as at all similar! So the account allows us to take the *b*-phase as cohering with the *c*-phase in Figure 1 while disallowing the coherence claim in the second case. The account also matches observations of certain amnesics: some motor or pattern recognition skills acquired during Pamela's *b*-phase in the Figure 1 situation may well persist into the *c*-phase, even though she has no apparent recollection of acquiring or previously practising these skills. But it would be entirely puzzling if such skills were passed from the branch to the main line person.

IV. Conclusion

The co-consciousness theorist who sees amnesia as a crucial problem for the Lockean analysis should not despair too soon. The modified account proposed in this paper seems to have a certain promise. I have, of course, not gone into detail about the qualifications the three conditions must have if they are to cope with various problems. Nor have I time to consider Lewis's suggestion that '(at least in some respects) there should not be too much change overall.' If he is right, then the ascription of two episodes to the life of one person might be

---

13 Or whatever we are supposed to say in such a bizarre case; see Dennett's 'Where am I?' in *Brainstorms*.

defeated on the grounds that they do not show enough coherence and connectedness under the three conditions. Importantly, the account suggests that coherence can come in degrees. It is typical of the healthy person that a project or hobby laid aside at one time can be taken up at another, or that an intention can lie dormant for some time before being acted upon. I have not tried to specify any plausible degree of coherence in terms of our three conditions that would definitely constitute identity. Further investigation may well show that there is no one way of doing this compatible with our various beliefs about personal identity. Moreover, I have tried to stay neutral on the identity issue itself. Rather, the suggested conditions provide a framework within which we can argue about the amount of change compatible with – and the amount of shared material and structure necessary to – that unity typical of one person's life. So Lewis, Parfit and Wiggins might well agree in using the three conditions while disagreeing about the degree to which each condition typically holds in one life. For example, the conditions permit us to argue that the amnesic Pamela shows enough coherence among her experiences to allow us to assign them all to one person. At the same time, they permit the formulation of much stronger identity conditions that would rule out the claims of Pamela to be regarded as one person.

There is, interestingly, one striking dissimilarity between the key notion of *survival* as deployed by me and its use by Parfit. For him, survival seems sometimes like a kind of surrogate for identity, capturing all that is important in identity, but used in describing cases like fission where the presence of a rival rules out an identity claim. For Parfit, then, I survive as myself in the normal course of events. In my usage, however, survival is typically a relation between distinct things. It was the survival of each *separate* stage of a discontinuous object in (or as) its successor that underpinned the allocation of all the stages to one and the same object. Likewise, I have taken it to be a possibility that we can regard distinct episodes of consciousness as related by the survival relation: the further question has been whether we can allocate the episodes to one and the same person, perhaps Pamela. And my suggestion has been that we can consider the *degree* of such survival as crucial to any attempt to settle the identity issue.[14] Now the important thing to notice is that, unlike Parfit, I am not discussing *the survival of Pamela*. Survival, for Parfit, is of course related to the survival, as I see it, of one episode or stage as (or in) another. My own view is that we can make sense of one thing's surviving as another along the lines sketched here; but this does not lead me to be confident that personal survival, in Parfit's sense, is any more determinate than personal identity.

It may be that in the case of really gross amnesias – where, for example, the mechanism of retrieval itself no longer operates – there is no room for even the weakest sort of personal identity. A proper discussion of this kind of case would require further assessment of, among others, the body condition. None of the arguments in this paper are intended to be a direct challenge to that condition. Nor has it been my intention to suggest that the proposed conditions will through their application remove in the end the grounds for indeterminacy in our notions about identity – an indeterminacy drawn to our attention by the famous puzzle cases (see my paper mentioned in note 6). Instead, I have tried to show that amnesia (at least of certain sorts) is not itself one such puzzle.

Received August, 1983

---

14 I have some tentative suggestions on degree of survival in the *Synthese* paper mentioned in note 6.

NOTES ON CONTRIBUTORS

Jane McIntyre is Associate Professor of Philosophy at Cleveland State University. Her primary work has been in philosophy of mind, British philosophy of the seventeenth and eighteenth centuries, and combinations of those areas. Her work has appeared in *Nous, Philosophical Studies, Analysis,* and *Hume Studies.*

Keith Lehrer is Professor of Philosophy and Department Head at The University of Arizona at Tucson. He is author with J.W. Cornman and G.S. Pappas of *Philosophical Problems and Arguments: An Introduction,* 3rd Edition; *Knowledge*; and with C. Wagner, *Rational Consensus in Science and Society: A Philosophical and Mathematical Study.* He is also the subject of a book, *Keith Lehrer,* edited by R. Bogdan.

John-Christian Smith is an Instructor and Doctoral Candidate in Philosophy and Cognitive Science at The University of Arizona. He is past winner of the Reisen Prize for Best Essay in Philosophy and is completing a text on the historical foundations of Cognitive Science. His article 'Reid's Functional Explanation of Sensation' is forthcoming in *History of Philosophy Quarterly.*

Richard Sharvy works on metaphysics, philosophical logic, philosophy of language, Greek philosophy, and political philosophy. His articles have appeared in *The Journal of Philosophy, Nous, The Philosophical Review, Philosophical Studies, The Monist, Philosophy of Science, Philosophy and Phenomenological Research,* and *Playboy.*

William Lyons is Senior Lecturer in Philosophy at the University of Glasgow, Scotland. He is the author of *Emotion, Gilbert Ryle: An Introduction to his Philosophy,* and articles in philosophy of mind and philosophical psychology. He is at present doing research into the nature of introspection.

Janet Levin is Assistant Professor at the University of Southern California. Her interests include philosophy of mind, philosophy of psychology, and epistemology.

Jeffrey Foss is Assistant Professor in the Department of Philosophy at the University of Victoria, Canada. He has published papers in *American Philosophical Quarterly, Philosophy of Science,* and the *Canadian Journal of Philosophy.*

B. Thurston received a Ph.D. from the University of British Columbia in 1981 and taught there in 1981-82. From 1982-84 she held a Killam Postdoctoral Fellowship and was a Visiting Scholar at Stanford University. She is presently teaching at U.B.C. Earlier papers appeared in *Mind* and *Canadian Philosophical Reviews.* An other paper is forthcoming in *Synthese.*

S. Coval is Professor of Philosophy at the University of British Columbia. His most recent work (co-authored) is an application of action theory to the philosophy of law and is to be published this year.

Paul M. Churchland is a member of the Philosophy Department at the University of California, San Diego. He is the author of *Scientific Realism and the Plasticity of Mind* and *Matter and Consciousness.* He has published articles in many journals including *Philosophy of Science, Journal of Philosophy, The Philosophical Review, Pacific Philosophical Quarterly,* and the *Journal of Philosophy and Biology.*

Christopher Cherry is a Senior Lecturer in Philosophy at the University of Kent at Canterbury. He has published articles on a wide range of philosophical topics in various journals, including *Mind, Philosophy, Philosophical Quarterly, Ratio, Philosophy and Phenomenological Research,* and *Philosophical Investigations.*

Andrew Brennan is editor of the Scots Philosophical Monograph Series and teaches in the Philosophy Department at the University of Stirling. Recent publications of his have appeared in *Nous, Synthese, Analysis* and *Environmental Ethics.*